Contents

KV-493-070

Introduction

Who is this book for?

Get Ready for IELTS Speaking has been written for learners with a band score of 3 or 4 who want to achieve a higher score. Using this book will help you improve your pre-intermediate speaking skills for the IELTS Academic Speaking test.

You can use *Get Ready for IELTS Speaking*:

- as a self-study course. We recommend that you work systematically through the 12 units in order to benefit from its progressive structure.
- as a supplementary speaking skills course for IELTS preparation classes. The book provides enough material for approximately 50 hours of classroom activity.

Get Ready for IELTS Speaking

- This comprises a book and a CD.
- The book contains **12 units**. Each unit focuses on a different topic and these topics are ones that often appear in the IELTS exam.
- After every three units, there is a **Review unit** which helps you to revise the language and skills covered in the previous units.
- At the end of the book the **Practice test** gives you the opportunity to take an IELTS-style test under test conditions.
- There is also a full **answer key** at the back of the book so you can check your answers. Here you will find suggested answers for more open-ended questions and model answers for the exam practice questions in Part 3 of the unit.
- The **glossary** at the back of the book lists the useful words from each unit with their Cobuild dictionary definitions.
- The audio CD contains the listening exercises. When you see this icon ◀))) please play the CD.

Unit structure

Each unit starts with the **Aims** of the unit. They outline the key language and skills covered.

Part 1: Language development introduces vocabulary related to the topic, as well as phrases and language that can be applied to any topic. The vocabulary exercises give you the opportunity to express complex ideas and opinions so that you are able to do so in the IELTS Speaking test. In addition, each unit covers one or more pronunciation and grammar points. The pronunciation and grammar exercises help you to develop accurate pronunciation, and grammatical range and accuracy to enable you to succeed in the IELTS test.

Part 2: Skills development teaches you exam skills. The information and exercises help you to understand what a good IELTS answer is and also provide you with strategies on how to achieve this. Skills include making notes for Part 2 of the IELTS Speaking test, developing your fluency, and improving the length and quality of your answers to Part 3 of the test by using news articles.

Part 3: Exam practice gives you the opportunity to practise the new language you have learnt by attempting questions from Part 1, Part 2 and Part 3 of the IELTS Speaking test. These test questions increase your familiarity with the exam format and help build your confidence.

Finally, a **checklist** summarises the key points covered in the unit.

Collins
English for Exams

5&p

Get Ready for IELTS
SPEAKING

Rhona Snelling

Collins

HarperCollins Publishers
77-85 Fulham Palace Road
Hammersmith
London W6 8JB

First edition 2012

Reprint 10 9 8 7 6 5 4 3 2 1 0

© HarperCollins Publishers 2012

ISBN 978–0–00–746063–2

Collins® is a registered trademark of HarperCollins
Publishers Limited

www.collinselt.com

A catalogue record for this book is available from the
British Library

Typeset in India by Aptara

Printed in China by South China Printing Co.

About the author
Rhona Snelling is a freelance ELT writer and editor, with
extensive experience of teaching exam courses in private
language schools and universities in the UK and overseas.
She has a Master's degree in Applied Linguistics from the
University of Oxford.

Author's acknowledgements
For my family and my Andreas

Thank you to Catherine Whitaker, Celia Wigley and Lorna
McGavigan at HarperCollins, and to the brilliant editorial
team of Matthew Duffy and Sheila Dignen.

Other features

Exam information boxes in each unit provide key background information about the IELTS Speaking exam.

Exam tip boxes provide essential exam techniques and strategies.

Watch out! boxes highlight common errors in the exam.

Study tips

- Each unit contains approximately three hours of study material.
- Try to answer the questions without looking at a dictionary to develop the skill of guessing the meaning of unknown words from context. This is important because dictionaries cannot be used during the actual exam.
- Use a pencil to complete the exercises, so that you can erase your first answers and do the exercises again for revision.
- Try to revise what you have learnt in Parts 1 and 2 before doing the practice IELTS questions in Part 3. This will improve the quality of your answers, and using the new language will help you to remember it.
- It's recommended that you try and complete all questions in the unit as the skills needed to do well at the IELTS test can only be improved through extensive practice.
- Read the answer key carefully as this provides information on what kind of answer is awarded high marks.
- Listen to the sample answers on the CD and practise reading these out loud as you listen, copying the native speakers' pronunciation as closely as you can.
- Record your answers if you can. It will develop your self-awareness: you will be able to hear what you are good at and where you need to improve. Also, hearing how your speaking has improved over time will increase your confidence. Remember that there are no 'right' or 'wrong' answers to the exam questions: the examiner is interested in your English, not in testing the validity of your opinions.
- It is very important that you do not memorise entire sentences or answers. IELTS examiners are trained to spot this and will change the topic if they think you are repeating memorised answers.

Other titles

Also available in the *Collins Get Ready for IELTS* series: *Reading*, *Listening* and *Writing*.

The International English Language Testing System (IELTS) Test

IELTS is jointly managed by the British Council, Cambridge ESOL Examinations and IDP Education, Australia.

There are two versions of the test:

- Academic
- General Training

Academic is for students wishing to study at undergraduate or postgraduate levels in an English-medium environment.

General Training is for people who wish to migrate to an English-speaking country.

This book is primarily for students taking the Academic version.

The Test

There are four modules:

Listening	30 minutes, plus 10 minutes for transferring answers to the answer sheet NB: the audio is heard *only once*. Approx. 10 questions per section Section 1: two speakers discuss a social situation Section 2: one speaker talks about a non-academic topic Section 3: up to four speakers discuss an educational project Section 4: one speaker gives a talk of general academic interest
Reading	60 minutes 3 texts, taken from authentic sources, on general, academic topics. They may contain diagrams, charts, etc. 40 questions: may include multiple choice, sentence completion, completing a diagram, graph or chart, choosing headings, yes/no, true/false questions, classification and matching exercises.
Writing	Task 1: 20 minutes: description of a table, chart, graph or diagram (150 words minimum) Task 2: 40 minutes: an essay in response to an argument or problem (250 words minimum)
Speaking	11–14 minutes A three-part face-to-face oral interview with an examiner. The interview is recorded. Part 1: introductions and general questions (4–5 mins) Part 2: individual long turn (3–4 mins) – the candidate is given a task, has one minute to prepare, then talks for 1–2 minutes, with some questions from the examiner. Part 3: two-way discussion (4–5 mins): the examiner asks further questions on the topic from Part 2, and gives the candidate the opportunity to discuss more abstract issues or ideas.
Timetabling	Listening, Reading and Writing must be taken on the same day, and in the order listed above. Speaking can be taken up to 7 days before or after the other modules.
Scoring	Each section is given a band score. The average of the four scores produces the Overall Band Score. You do not pass or fail IELTS; you receive a score.

IELTS and the Common European Framework of Reference

The CEFR shows the level of the learner and is used for many English as a Foreign Language examinations.

The table below shows the approximate CEFR level and the equivalent IELTS Overall Band Score:

CEFR description	CEFR code	IELTS Band Score
Proficient user	C2	9
(Advanced)	C1	7–8
Independent user	B2	5–6.5
(Intermediate – Upper Intermediate)	B1	4–5

This table contains the general descriptors for the band scores 1–9:

IELTS Band Scores		
9	Expert user	Has fully operational command of the language: appropriate, accurate and fluent with complete understanding.
8	Very good user	Has fully operational command of the language, with only occasional unsystematic inaccuracies and inappropriacies. Misunderstandings may occur in unfamiliar situations. Handles complex detailed argumentation well.
7	Good user	Has operational command of the language, though with occasional inaccuracies, inappropriacies and misunderstandings in some situations. Generally handles complex language well and understands detailed reasoning.
6	Competent user	Has generally effective command of the language despite some inaccuracies, inappropriacies and misunderstandings. Can use and understand fairly complex language, particularly in familiar situations.
5	Modest user	Has partial command of the language, coping with overall meaning in most situations, though is likely to make many mistakes. Should be able to handle basic communication in own field.
4	Limited user	Basic competence is limited to familiar situations. Has frequent problems in understanding and expression. Is not able to use complex language.
3	Extremely limited user	Conveys and understands only general meaning in very familiar situations. Frequent breakdowns in communication occur.
2	Intermittent user	No real communication is possible except for the most basic information using isolated words or short formulae in familiar situations and to meet immediate needs. Has great difficulty understanding spoken and written English.
1	Non user	Essentially has no ability to use the language beyond possibly a few isolated words.
0	Did not attempt the test	No assessable information provided.

Marking

The Listening and Reading papers have 40 items, each worth one mark if correctly answered. Here are some examples of how marks are translated into band scores:

Listening:
16 out of 40 correct answers: band score 5
23 out of 40 correct answers: band score 6
30 out of 40 correct answers: band score 7

Reading
15 out of 40 correct answers: band score 5
23 out of 40 correct answers: band score 6
30 out of 40 correct answers: band score 7

Writing and Speaking are marked according to performance descriptors.
Writing: examiners award a band score for each of four areas with equal weighting:

- Task achievement (Task 1)
- Task response (Task 2)
- Coherence and cohesion
- Lexical resource and grammatical range and accuracy

Speaking: examiners award a band score for each of four areas with equal weighting:

- Fluency and coherence
- Lexical resource
- Grammatical range
- Accuracy and pronunciation

For full details of how the examination is scored and marked, go to: www.ielts.org

1 Family

AIMS: Talking about family • Describing people • Pronunciation: /ð/ • Possessive adjectives • Skills development: Understanding Part 1 • Exam practice: Part 1

Part 1: Language development

Vocabulary: Family

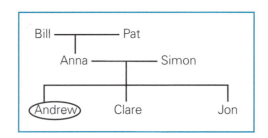

1 Look at Andrew's family tree. Complete the sentences with the words below.

> brothers   daughter   grandparents   husband   mother   parents   sister   sons   wife

> **1** Clare is Andrew's ....
>
> **2** Andrew and Jon are Clare's ....
>
> **3** Andrew's .... are called Simon and Anna.
>
> **4** Anna is Andrew's .... and Simon's ....
>
> **5** Simon and Anna have three children – one .... and two ....
>
> **6** Pat and Bill are Andrew's .... Bill is Pat's ....

2 Read and complete the text about Andrew's family.

> My name's Andrew. I've got one (1) .... Her name is Clare. I've got one (2) .... His name's Jon. He's a student. My (3) ....'s name is Anna and she's a teacher. My (4) ....'s name is Simon and he's a doctor.

Watch Out!

Use the contraction **'s** in spoken English.

My name's Andrew.   ~~My name is Andrew.~~

---

3 Rewrite the text in Exercise 2 to describe your family.

Pronunciation: /ð/

🔊 **4** Listen and repeat each word. The words below use the phonetic alphabet. This shows you
01   how to pronounce the words. Can you pronounce the /ð/ sound?

brother /ˈbrʌðə/   father /ˈfɑːðə/   grandfather /ˈgrændfɑːðə/

🔊 **5** Listen and repeat each word. Then listen again and write each word.
02

/ˈbrʌðə/ ....   /ˈmʌðə/ ....   /ˈgrændmʌðə/ ....

Vocabulary: Describing people

6 Find nine personality adjectives below. Use your dictionary to help you. Which can describe you?

bossycalinclevercconfidentcreativefriendlyfunnyhappykind

7 Complete the descriptions below with personality adjectives from Exercise 6.

1 My mother understands new things quickly. She's very ....
2 My father is very .... He tells me what to do every day.
3 I'm .... because I believe in my ability. For example, I'm good at speaking English!
4 My sister is never angry or worried. She's always ....
5 My brother is .... He enjoys meeting people. He's .... too. He always makes people laugh.

🔊 **8** Listen to three people describing someone in their family. Write the personality adjectives
03   that each speaker uses.

Speaker 1   ....
Speaker 2   ....
Speaker 3   ....

🔊 **9** Listen again. Complete the gaps with the words you hear. Use the audio script on page 89 to
03   check your answers.

Speaker 1   She .... like her sister. They've both got curly hair.
Speaker 2   I don't have any .... or sisters. I'm an only child.
Speaker 3   But their son is really funny! He's my .... cousin.

10 Describe someone in your family. Use personality adjectives and include extra information.

Grammar: Possessive adjectives

🔊 04 11 How would you describe your family? Read the description of Antony's family. Listen and complete the gaps with the words you hear.

My family? Well, we're a big family actually. (1) .... house is large! I've got five brothers. (2) .... names are Carlos, Gino, Luca, Alex and Marco. Carlos is 14 and he's the youngest. He's good looking and very funny. Marco is 27 and he's the oldest. (3) .... wife teaches at my college. (4) .... name is Maria.

My mother is an only child, so (5) .... family is very small. But (6) .... father is from a big family. He has three brothers. He looks like his brother, my uncle Georgio. They are both bossy but kind. My uncle has four children and one cat. (7) .... name is Lola. Tell me about (8) .... family.

Watch Out!

look like = have the same appearance

I look like my mother.

He looks like his father.

They look like their father.

12 Complete the table below.

....	you	he	....	it	....	they
my	....	....	her	....	our	....

13 Answer the questions below. Write full sentences.

1 Do you have any brothers or sisters? What are their names?
   Example: Yes, I have two sisters. Their names are Ela and Liz.

2 What is your father's name?

3 Who do you look like in your family? What is his/her name?

4 Have you got a pet? What is its name?

5 Who makes you laugh in your family?

6 Is someone in your family bossy?

14 Add one more sentence to your answers in Exercise 13.

Example: *1 Yes, I have two sisters. Their names are Ela and Liz. Ela looks like my mother and they are both very kind.*

15 How would you describe your family? Record your answer.

Part 2: Skills development

Exam information

The complete Speaking test takes 11–14 minutes. The examiner asks questions and you give answers. The answers are recorded.

Part 1: Introduction and interview

- Part 1 takes 4–5 minutes.
- In the introduction, the examiner introduces himself/herself to you. The examiner asks you to confirm your identity.
- Then the interview starts. The examiner asks you questions on general topics, e.g. family, hobbies, studying.
- Part 1 tests your ability to give full answers and to give extra information on general topics with descriptions or explanations.

1 **Read the Part 1 questions 1–5 below. Match each question with the correct topic a–e.**

1	Are you a student?	**a**	Your country
2	Describe your family.	**b**	Your family
3	Which country are you from?	**c**	Your hobbies
4	What do you do?	**d**	Your studies
5	Do you do any sports?	**e**	Your work

Watch Out!

What **do** you do? = What is your **job**?

2 🔊 05 **Read and listen to the examiner's instructions in Part 1. Complete the gaps.**

Hello. My (1) .... is Steve Smith. Could you tell me your (2) ...., please?

Thank you. Can you show me your (3) ...., please?

I'd now like to ask you some questions about yourself.

Tell me about your (4) ....

What does your father (5) .... ?

(6) .... much time do you spend with your family?

Are people in your (7) .... close to their family?

Do you prefer to go out with your family or your (8) .... ?

Where do you (9) .... at the moment?

3 🔊 06 **Listen to a candidate answering a question from Exercise 2. Which question is it?**

◀)) 4 Listen to the candidate's answer again and assess it. Choose the best description.
06

    1 The information in the answer is *relevant / not relevant*.

    2 The answer is *very short / OK / very long*.

    3 The candidate speaks *with pauses / at normal speed / very fast*.

    4 The vocabulary is *relevant / not relevant* to the topic.

    5 The pronunciation is *poor / OK / clear*.

    6 There are *a lot of errors / one or two errors / no errors* in the grammar.

5 Record your answer to the same question.

6 Listen to your answer and assess it. Choose the best description.

    1 The information in the answer is *relevant / not relevant*.

    2 The answer is *very short / OK / very long*.

    3 I speak *with pauses / at normal speed / very fast*.

    4 The vocabulary is *relevant / not relevant* to the topic.

    5 The pronunciation is *poor / OK / clear*.

    6 There are *a lot of errors / one or two errors / no errors* in the grammar.

7 How can you improve your answer? Choose one or two pieces of advice below to improve your answer. Then record your answer again.

    • Give a longer answer. Practise giving answers that are two or three full sentences.

    • Imagine you are speaking to a friend and speak at your normal speed – not fast and not slow.

    • Go back to the Vocabulary sections and learn more words for family.

    • Go back to the Pronunciation section or use your dictionary and practise saying difficult words.

    • Go back to the Grammar section and check you understand everything.

8 Choose one more question from Exercise 2 and record your answer. Assess your answer, then try to improve it.

> ## Exam tip
> The questions in Part 1 are on general topics about <u>your</u> life. Your answers are from your life and experience. There is no right or wrong answer.

Part 3: Exam practice

1 Read the Part 1 questions. Record your answers to the questions.

    1 Which country are you from?
    2 Do you have a large family?
    3 What does your mother do?
    4 Do you live with your family?

2 Listen to three more Part 1 questions. Write the questions. Then record your answers.

07

    1 ....
    2 ....
    3 ....

Progress check

3 Listen to your answers to Exercises 1 and 2. Tick the boxes below to assess your answers.

Do you ...
give a long answer? ☐
speak at a normal speed? ☐
use vocabulary for describing people? ☐
use correct pronunciation? ☐
use possessive adjectives correctly? ☐

2 Free time

Part 1: Language development

Vocabulary: Free time activities

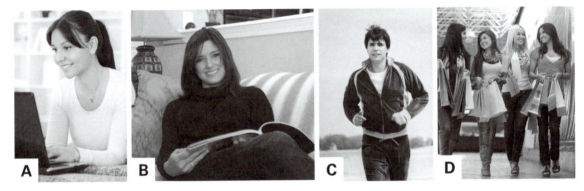

1 Match the photos A–D to four of the activities below.

> going shopping   jogging   listening to music   playing computer games
> chatting online   playing tennis   reading magazines   watching a film

2 Complete the table with the nouns below. How many activities can you make?

> a DVD   exercise   football   to the gym   nothing   for walks   tennis   TV

doing	
going	
playing	
watching	

3 What do you think about the activities in Exercises 1 and 2? Write each activity next to an adjective. Can you add any more activities?

1 boring ....*doing nothing*..

2 relaxing ....

3 interesting ....

4 exciting ....

4 Write sentences for each activity. Use *I like …* / *I don't like …* and an adjective from Exercise 3.

Example: *I don't like playing computer games. I think it's very boring.*

Vocabulary: Expressing preferences

5 Listen to three people answering the question 'What do you like doing in your free time?' What does each speaker enjoy doing? Write the activities from the box.

08

> doing nothing   going for walks   going shopping
>   playing computer games   reading magazines   ~~using the Internet~~

Speaker 1	Speaker 2	Speaker 3
using the Internet		

6 Listen to extracts from the answers in Exercise 6. Complete the gaps with the phrases below.

09

> I don't like   I love   I prefer   I really like   It depends   My favourite thing

1 .... using the Internet.
2 .... chatting online with him.
3 .... doing nothing to doing exercise.
4 .... going to the gym.
5 .... Sometimes I like going for walks.
6 .... is going shopping.

Watch Out!

We can use *really* + verb to give emphasis.   **We cannot use *very* + verb.**

I really like going to the cinema.   ~~I very like going to the cinema.~~

7 Write a short answer to the question 'What do you like doing?' Use the phrases from Exercise 6 and the audio script on page 89 to help you.

Grammar: Present simple

8 Read the rule and look at the table. Use the information to choose the correct answer (a or b) to questions 1–5.

- Use the present simple to make general statements about your life.

	+	−
I	like	don't like
You	like	don't like
He / She / It	likes	doesn't like
We / You / They	like	don't like

1 Does your best friend play tennis?

    a No, he doesn't play tennis but he likes playing computer games.

    b No, he not play tennis but he likes playing computer games.

2 Do you watch DVDs?

    a Yes. I likes watch DVDs at the weekend. But I don't like watching TV.

    b Yes. I like watching DVDs at the weekend. But I don't like watching TV.

3 Tell me about something you like doing.

    a I liking go to museums. It's very interesting.

    b I like going to museums. It's very relaxing.

4 Do you do any exercise?

    a Yes, I go to the gym every morning at 6 a.m.

    b Yes, I going to the gym every morning at 6 a.m.

5 Do you like reading newspapers?

    a It depends. Sometimes I read the newspapers on Saturdays.

    b It depends. Sometimes I liking the newspapers on Saturdays.

9 Answer each of the questions in Exercise 8.

Watch Out!

on + *day*: on Saturdays

at + *time*: at 6 a.m.

at + *the weekend*: at the weekend

Use **every** to say how often you do something: every morning

Part 2: Skills development

Exam information

The complete Speaking test (Parts 1, 2 and 3) takes 11–14 minutes. The examiner asks questions and the candidate gives answers. The answers are recorded.

Part 2: Individual long turn

- Part 2 takes 3–4 minutes.
- The examiner gives you a 'task card' with written prompts. The examiner asks you to talk about the topic and include the points on the card. The topic is about a personal experience.
- You have one minute to prepare your talk, and the examiner gives you a pencil and paper to make notes.
- You talk for one to two minutes about the topic. You can use your notes to help you.
- Then the examiner asks you one or two more questions on the same topic.
- Part 2 tests your ability to talk about a topic, develop your ideas about a topic, and relevant vocabulary and grammar.

🔊 **1**
10
Listen to the examiner's instructions for the task card below. What newspaper or magazine do you enjoy reading? What is the title?

> **Describe a <u>newspaper or magazine</u> you enjoy reading.**
>
> You should say:
>
> <u>what kind</u> of newspaper or magazine it is
> <u>which parts</u> of it you read
> <u>when</u> and <u>where</u> you read it
>
> and <u>explain why</u> you enjoy reading it.

🔊 **2**
11
Notice the <u>underlined</u> key words on the task card. Read the notes on each key word below. Listen to a model answer. Circle the notes that the speaker talks about.

1	newspaper or magazine:	(magazine) | newspaper
2	what kind:	fashion | sport | travel
3	which parts:	adverts | interviews | letters | news
4	when:	every day | the weekend | sometimes
5	where:	home | school
6	explain why:	It's very interesting. | It's relaxing.

🔊 **3**
11

Match the sentences below to the key words in Exercise 2. Listen again and check.

    a I enjoy reading a magazine called *Fab Football*. *newspaper or magazine*

    b I prefer reading the interviews with famous players or the news. ....

    c I read *Fab Football* every weekend. ....

    d It's about sport. ....

    e It's very interesting. ....

    f Then I go home and read. ....

4 **Look back at the task card in Exercise 1 and prepare your answer. Make notes for each key word.**

    1 newspaper or magazine: ....

    2 what kind: ....

    3 which parts: ....

    4 when: ....

    5 where: ....

    6 explain why: ....

5 **Make sentences from your notes. Use Exercise 3 to help you.**

    1 newspaper or magazine: ....

    2 what kind: ....

    3 which parts: ....

    4 when: ....

    5 where: ....

    6 explain why: ....

6 **Record your answer to the task card in Exercise 1. Use your notes to help you.**

Part 3: Exam practice

🔊 **1** Read the task card below and listen to the examiner's instructions. Underline the key words.
12

> **Describe an activity you like doing.**
>
> You should say:
>
> **what activity is it**
> **where and when you do you do it**
> **who you like doing it with**
>
> And explain why you enjoy doing it.

2 Plan your answer. Write notes for each of the key words. You have one minute for this in the exam.

3 Record your answer. You have one to two minutes for this in the exam.

Progress check

4 Listen to your answer. Tick the boxes below to assess your answers.

Do you …
talk about all the key words on the task card? ☐
use vocabulary for expressing preferences? ☐
use vocabulary for free time activities? ☐
use the present simple? ☐

3 Special occasions

Part 1: Language development

Vocabulary: Special occasions

A   B   C

1   **Look at the photos of special occasions. Which of the things in the box below can you see?**

balloons	cake	cards	carnival	costume	family
fireworks	friends	parade	presents	traditional food	

2   **Complete the descriptions of special occasions with the words below.**

family	give	make	presents

In my country, we celebrate name days. We (1) .... cards and (2) ....
traditional food. I enjoy visiting my (3) .... on my name day and I love receiving
(4) ....!

fireworks	parade	watch	wear

New Year is a very special occasion. There's a (5) .... through the streets and
people (6) .... beautiful costumes. We (7) .... the parade and we
celebrate the start of a new year with (8) ....

Vocabulary: Connecting ideas

🔊 **3** Read the description of Steven's trip. Put a–f in gaps 1–6. Then listen and check.
13

> **a** It was a special trip for me **because** ...
> **b** **but** it wasn't very nice.
> **c** it was very exciting!
> **d** My best friend went **too**.
> **e** **Then** we visited another city
> **f** we walked to the city centre.

Last year I travelled to Rio and visited my cousin and his family. (1) .... We went to my cousin's house and we had a delicious traditional meal. **After** we ate dinner, (2) .... **When** we saw the carnival, (3) .... We danced and sang. We watched the parade. It was fun, but we were very tired. (4) .... and stayed at a famous hotel (5) .... We stayed for two days then we went home. (6) .... I travelled without my parents for the first time.

4 Look at the bold words in Exercise 3. Then choose the correct word to complete the sentences.

1 I enjoyed the parade and the carnival, *but / because* I was very tired.
2 We went to a local restaurant for lunch, *then / but* we went to visit some friends.
3 I got a present from my parents. I got a present from my brother *after / too*.
4 *After / When* the graduation ceremony, my family met my friends from university.
5 I didn't enjoy the trip *too / because* I don't like travelling by bus.
6 *When / but* the fireworks started, we were very excited.

Grammar: Past simple

5 Read the rules and look at the table. Complete the past simple form of the irregular verbs below. Use your dictionary to help you.

- Use the past simple for past actions that are finished.
- For regular verbs, add *–d* or *–ed*.
- For irregular verbs, learn the different forms.
- For the verb *be*, learn the different forms for different persons.

	Infinitive	Past simple +	Past simple –
Regular verbs	dance	danced	didn't dance
Irregular verbs	sing	sang	didn't sing
The verb *be*	be	was / were	wasn't / weren't

1 eat ....
2 give ....
3 make ....
4 meet ....
5 wear ....
6 see ....

6 Complete the sentences with the words below.

> danced   didn't stay   graduated   was   went   were

  1 I wasn't at the carnival. I .... to my sister's wedding.
  2 I .... last year. My parents came to England for the ceremony.
  3 People wore colourful costumes. It .... an exciting day!
  4 We watched the parade. We sang and .... to the music.
  5 I stayed with my friends. I .... in a hotel.
  6 We didn't see the fireworks. We .... tired and went to the hotel.

Pronunciation: Past simple verbs and -ed

🔊 **7** The -ed ending is pronounced in three different ways. Listen to the different sounds and the
14 past simple verbs in the table below.

/t/	/d/	/ɪd/
danced watched	stayed travelled	hated visited

🔊 **8** Listen to six past simple verbs and add them to the table above.
15

> ## Watch Out!
>
> The -ed ending adds a sound to the end. Sometimes it adds an extra syllable to
> the verb.
>
> For example:
> dance + -ed = danced (one syllable)
> hate + -ed = ha-ted (two syllables)

9 Complete the sentences with the words below. Use the correct form of the verbs.

  1 > but   meet   travel   watch

   I .... my friends in the park after the carnival. We .... the fireworks
   and .... home. We had a great time, ... we were very tired.

  2 > see   play   wear   when

   My hometown has a big festival each year. Last year, I .... a costume
   and .... traditional music at the parade. My parents were very
   happy .... they .... the parade.

Part 2: Skills development

1 Look at beginnings of Part 2 task cards 1–3. Match each card with a general topic a–c.

1

> **Describe someone in your family who you like.**
>
> You should say:
>
> **what kind of person he/she is**

2

> **Describe an activity that you like doing.**
>
> You should say:
>
> **what activity is it**

3

> **Describe a special occasion in your life.**
>
> You should say:
>
> **where this occasion took place**

- **a** events ....
- **b** hobbies ....
- **c** people ....

2 Now match each question a–c with a task card 1–3 from Exercise 1.

- **a** Do young people in your country celebrate special occasions? ....
- **b** What do you think are the differences between sports now and in the past? ....
- **c** What is the role of grandparents in your culture? ....

Exam tip

The Part 2 task prepares you for Part 3 because you talk about a related topic.

◀)) **3**
16

Look at the <u>underlined</u> key words in the Part 3 question below. Listen to two more Part 3 questions. Write the questions and underline the key words.

Do <u>you think</u> <u>computer games</u> are <u>good</u>?

1 ....

2 ....

◀)) **4**
16

Listen again and check.

5   Read the model answers to a question in Exercise 3. Which question do the answers match?

a

Yes, I think, yes. In my country, we have one or two big festivals. We visit family or we remember people or events. It is important. It is a serious thing but it is fun. I like travelling to other countries for festivals too. It is interesting to learn about the world.

b

I went to a festival in my country last year and I enjoyed it. It was important to me because I saw my friends and family.

6   Look at the model answers in Exercise 5 again. Answer the questions below for each model answer.

1   Is the answer on the same general topic?
2   Is it relevant to the question?
3   Does it include the key words or words similar to the key words?
4   How long is the answer?

Exam tip

Try to give an answer with four or more sentences. Do not give short answers.

7   Choose a Part 3 question from Exercise 2 or Exercise 3 and write your own answer.

8   Record your answer, then use the questions in Exercise 6 to check your answer.

Part 3: Exam practice

Part 2

1 Read the Part 2 task card below and write notes for your answer. You have one minute for this in the exam.

> **Describe a special occasion in your life**
>
> You should say:
>
> **where this occasion took place**
> **when it took place**
> **who was there**
>
> and explain how your feelings on this occasion.

2 Record your answer. You have one to two minutes for this in the exam.

Part 3

🔊 **3** Read and listen to the Part 3 questions.
17

> What is an important festival in your country?
> What are your favourite parts of this festival?
> How have special occasions such as weddings changed in your country?
> Do you think special occasions and festivals are important for a society?

4 Record your answers to each question in Exercise 3.

Progress check

5 Listen to your answers. Tick the boxes below to assess your answers.

Do you …
talk about all the key words on the task card in Part 2? ☐
talk about the right topic in Part 3? ☐
answer with four or more sentences in Part 3? ☐
use vocabulary for special occasions? ☐
use vocabulary for connecting ideas? ☐
use the past simple? ☐
use correct pronunciation for past simple -*ed* endings? ☐

Review 1

1 Complete the table with family words.

mother	wife	(2)	sister	(4)	granddaughter
father	(1)	son	(3)	grandfather	(5) ....

2 Circle the correct word to describe people.

1 A *funny / kind* person cares about other people.
2 A *bossy / friendly* person tells other people what to do.
3 A *calm / creative* person uses their imagination to make new things.
4 A *confident / happy* person believes in their ability.
5 A *clever / friendly* person likes meeting new people.

3 Complete the sentences with possessive adjectives in the box.

her	his	our	my (x2)	your

1 .... name is Abdul. I am 19 years old.
2 Is .... family big or small?
3 My grandmother is 80. .... name is Ana.
4 I'm not an only child. This is .... sister Maria.
5 My husband is from Australia. .... relatives still live there.

4 Read the sentences about free time activities. Cross out the incorrect options below. There is one incorrect option in each sentence.

1 My favourite thing is playing *computer games / tennis / the Internet*.
2 I really like chatting online. It's *boring / exciting / relaxing*.
3 I don't like watching *DVDs / films / magazines*.
4 I love doing *exercise / to the gym / nothing*
5 I prefer going *shopping / to the gym / to music*.

5 Listen and choose the correct sentence (a or b).

18

1 **a** It's boring.   **b** It's interesting

2 **a** I like doing nothing.   **b** I like doing exercise.

3 **a** I don't like using the internet.   **b** I like using the internet.

6 Correct the errors with the present simple in the sentences below.

1 I like really playing computer games.

2 Children in my country don't like go shopping.

3 My brother and I likes going to museums.

4 I no like going for walks.

7 Complete the time expressions with the correct preposition: *at* or *on*.

1 I like doing nothing .... the weekend.

2 I play tennis .... Saturday.

3 I go to the gym .... 6 a.m. every day.

8 Match the verbs with the words in the box below to describe special occasions.

give   visit   watch   wear

a costume   family   fireworks   presents

9 Connect the ideas in the sentences with the best word.

1 The journey was very long, *b* .... I was excited and happy.

2 We saw the parade on Saturday. *T* .... we visited friends on Sunday.

3 *A* .... the fireworks, I went home. I was very tired.

4 I made traditional food for my family. My mother made some food *t* ....

5 *W* .... I arrived at the restaurant, all my family were there.

6 We wore new clothes *b* .... it was special day.

10 Complete the sentences with the past simple form of the verbs in brackets.

1 I .... England last summer. It .... great. (visit, is)

2 My parents .... at the parade, but they .... it. (are, not like)

3 We .... and .... at the carnival. (sing, dance)

4 I .... last year and .... my first job. (graduate, get)

5 I .... to the restaurant because I .... very tired. (not go, is)

4 Hometown

AIMS: Talking about places in cities • Describing cities • Pronunciation: Syllables and word stress
• *There is/There are* • Skills development: Building fluency • Exam practice: Part 1 and Part 2

Part 1: Language development

Vocabulary: Places in cities

A   B   C

1 **Match photos A–C to the places below. There are three extra places.**

> football stadium   gallery   harbour   market   museum   shopping mall

2 **Look at the photos again. What can you do in each place? Choose activities from the list.**

> buy clothes   go on a boat trip   have a coffee   see an exhibition

Example: *You can buy clothes in a shopping mall.*

3 **In which place below can you do activites 1–5? Can you add more places?**

> beach   bridge   café   factory   gallery   hotel   park   river   skyscraper   theatre

  1 eat or drink something
  2 go for a walk
  3 relax and meet friends
  4 work
  5 see a view of the city

Vocabulary: Describing cities

4   Match the meanings of sentences 1–5 with a–e.

1   It's a <u>busy</u> city.

2   It's near the <u>beach</u>.

3   It's got <u>different neighbourhoods</u>.

4   It is famous for the <u>markets</u>.

5   I really like it because <u>the people are very friendly</u>.

a   I go swimming there at the weekend. Sometimes we go sailing too.

b   They are polite and they're very happy when you speak their language.

c   There's a lot of traffic and people say the city never sleeps!

d   Tourists buy clothes or souvenirs. You can even go on tours.

e   There's a financial district, a busy downtown and quiet suburbs.

5   Replace the <u>underlined</u> words and phrases in Exercise 4 to make more sentences about cities. Use the ideas below or your own ideas.

> airport   beautiful   museums   mountains   traditional food
> lots of tourist attractions   modern   the weather is good

Example: *It's a modern city.*

6   Complete the sentences below so they are true for your hometown.

1   It's a .... city.

2   It's near the …

3   It's got …

4   It is famous for the …

5   I really like it because …

Pronunciation: Syllables and word stress

🔊 **7**
19

Look at the words in Exercise 3 again. How many syllables (different word parts) are there? Complete the table, then listen and check.

one syllable	two syllables	three syllables
beach	*café*	

🔊 **8**
20

Listen to the words again and underline the syllable with the word stress.

Grammar: *There is/There are*

9 Listen to Sam describing a city. Write the words below next to the correct heading.

21

> accommodation   beach   harbours   markets
> museum   people   shopping malls   traffic

There's *a museum* ....
There isn't ....
There are ....
There aren't ....

10 Complete the table with the correct words.

+	There	's (is)	a museum.	
		(1)	some galleries.	
–	There	(2) .... / is not	a beach.	
		aren't / (3)	any harbours.	
?	Is	there	a football stadium?	Yes, there is. (5) ...., there isn't.
	(4)		any shopping malls?	Yes, there (6) .... No, there (7) ....

Watch Out!

Countable nouns have two forms:

There is a museum. (singular)

There are two museums. (plural)

Uncountable nouns have one form:

There isn't any accommodation.

~~There aren't any accommodations.~~

11 Read the text and complete each paragraph with the correct words.

> bridge   famous   got   near   skyscrapers

My hometown is (1) .... the border. It's a busy city and it's (2) ....
for the different neighbourhoods. It's (3) .... a financial district with lots of tall
(4) .... You can walk over a modern (5) .... into the harbour.

> are   can   favourite   meet   traditional

My (6) .... place is the historic centre. You (7) .... go to lots of small
restaurants and eat (8) .... food. It's delicious! It's a great place to
(9) .... friends. There (10) .... always lots of people there. It's a
popular place.

Part 2: Skills development

Exam information

Part 1 tests your ability to talk to people about everyday topics.

Part 2 tests your ability to talk about a specific topic and to organize your ideas.

Part 1

Exam tip

Try to give long answers – not just two or three words.

Speak at a natural speed – not fast and not slow – without lots of pauses.

Use synonyms and show your vocabulary.

Practise your grammar to help you use the correct forms.

1 Read the Part 1 question and answer below. What are the good and bad points about the answer?

A: How would you describe your hometown?

B: Busy. Dirty. I don't like it.

2 Prepare your answer to the question in Exercise 1. Make notes on the ideas below.

- location of the city (area? country?) and size (population?)
- positive words to describe a city
- places tourists visit
- your opinion and an example

3 Record your answer to the question. Use your notes to help you.

4 Listen to a model answer. Assess the answer in the table below.

22

	model answer	your answer
Is the answer too slow or too fast?		
Are there pauses?		
Are there any grammar errors?		
Are words repeated?		

5 Now listen to your answer and complete the table above.

6 How can you improve your answer? Record your answer again and try to improve your technique and language.

Part 2

Exam tip

In Part 2 of the exam, use the one minute to think and plan.

Identify the topic on the card.

Make notes on the three points and the summary point. This organizes your answer.

Choose topic vocabulary and suitable grammar structures.

Then speak at a natural speed for two minutes.

7 Read the Part 2 topic card and the candidate's notes below. Which notes are not useful? Why?

Describe an area of your country you know and like.

You should say:

where it is
what its special features are
what you and other people do in this area

And explain why you like it.

---

name of city (English translation?)

description of country

It's near ...

It's got ... / There's ...

tourists – try food, take photos

me – relax, meet friends, play sports

other cities I like

my opinion and example

---

8 Prepare your answer to the Part 2 task in Exercise 7. You have one minute to make notes. Use the Exam tip box to help you.

9 Look at your notes again. Can you improve them? Now record your answer. You have two minutes to give your answer.

10 Listen to your answer. Did you follow the points in the Exam tip box? How can you improve? Record your answer again for extra practice.

Part 3: Exam practice

Part 1

🔊 **1** **23** Read the Part 1 questions below. Then listen and match the answers a–g to the questions.

    1 Do you work or are you a student? ....

    2 What do you like about your job? / What do you like about studying? ....

    3 When do you see your friends and family? ....

    4 Where is your hometown located? ....

    5 What do people in your town do? ....

    6 Is it easy to travel around your hometown? ....

    7 Is there a good health system where you live? ....

2 Record your answers to the questions in Exercise 1.

Part 2

3 Read the instructions for the Part 2 topic card below. You have one minute to make notes for your answer.

> **Describe an interesting city you know and like.**
>
> You should say:
>
> **where it is**
> **how you went there**
> **what you did there**
>
> And explain why you found it so interesting.

4 Now record your answer to the task in Exercise 3. You have two minutes to give your answer.

Progress check

5 Listen to your answers to Part 1 and Part 2. Tick the boxes below to assess your answers.

Part 1		Part 2	
Do you ...		Do you ...	
give extra information or an example?	☐	keep talking and not have too many pauses?	☐
use topic vocabulary and phrases?	☐	use topic vocabulary and useful phrases?	☐
use the correct stress for the words?	☐	use the correct stress for the words ?	☐
use correct grammar?	☐	use correct grammar?	☐
		sound interested in the city?	☐

5 TV and radio

AIMS: Talking about types of TV and radio programme • Describing programmes • Adverbs of frequency • Skills development: Organizing your answers • Exam practice: Part 1 and Part 2

Part 1: Language development

Vocabulary: Types of programme

A B C D

1 Read the descriptions 1–6 of different types of programme. Match the descriptions with the photos A–D above. There are two extra descriptions.

1 I love watching documentaries because we can learn about new things. My favourite is a <u>series</u> about nature and animals.

2 I watch a game show every weekend with my family. I think the <u>presenter</u> is very funny. I like it when the contestants win big prizes.

3 I always listen to the news. I think it's important to understand the events in your country and listen to business reports. You can find out about your sports team too.

4 I enjoy watching soap operas because they are similar to real life and I like the <u>characters</u>. I usually watch TV on my laptop in my room.

5 I sometimes watch talk shows. The <u>guests</u> are really interesting. You can learn about their lives and new films or new music.

6 I'm a sports fan so I watch a lot of sport on TV. I enjoy listening to the experts talking about the results, too.

2 Check the meaning of the <u>underlined</u> words in Exercise 1. Then answer the questions below.

1 Do you have a favourite TV <u>presenter</u> Why do you like him/her?

2 What is a popular documentary <u>series</u> in your country?

3 Are there any <u>characters</u> in a soap opera you really like?

4 Do you think most <u>guests</u> on a talk show are interesting?

Vocabulary: Describing programmes

🔊 **3**
24

Listen to three people talking about programmes they listen to or watch. Match the speakers 1–3 with the type of programme they watch a–c.

    a documentary series ....
    b drama series ....
    c reality TV show ....

🔊 **4**
24

Read the sentences a–h below. Listen again and decide which speaker 1–3 says each sentence. Which three sentences express an opinion?

    a It's about clothes and fashion. ....
    b It's set in London. ....
    c It's presented by different models each week. ....
    d It stars some famous actors. ....
    e The participants are famous people. ....
    f It's very exciting. ....
    g I think it's good entertainment. ....
    h The thing I like best is the hotel manager. ....

5

Think about a programme you enjoy watching or listening to. Write sentences to describe it and express your opinion about it. Use the sentences in Exercise 5 to help you.

> ## Watch Out!
> **actors** = people who play characters in a story
> **characters** = people in a story
> **contestants** = real people in a game show or reality TV show

Grammar: Adverbs of frequency

6

Match sentences 1–6 to explanations a–f. Which sentences are true for you?

1 I always watch soap operas.

2 I usually listen to the news in the morning.

3 I often watch game shows.

4 I sometimes watch dramas.

5 I rarely listen to sports programmes.

6 I never watch documentaries.

a I'm not interested in any sports.

b I think they're very boring.

c I like it when contestants win big prizes.

d I think the plots are sometimes interesting.

e I watch them every day. I never miss an episode.

f I like listening to the business reports.

7 Look at the arrow and the adverbs of frequency. Put the words *always, often* and *rarely* in the correct position on the arrow.

never   (1) ....   sometimes   (2) ....   usually   (3) .... →

> ## Watch Out!
>
> Put the adverb **before** the verb: I always watch soap operas.
>
> BUT put the adverb **after** the verb *to be*: I think the plots are sometimes interesting.

8 Complete the prompts below so that they are true for you. Include an explanation.

   1 I always watch …
       Example: *I always watch dramas. I think they're exciting and I like the plots.*
   2 I usually listen to …
   3 I often watch …
   4 I sometimes watch …
   5 I rarely listen to …
   6 I never watch …

9 Complete the texts with the words below.

1

| by | contestants | every | favourite |

My .... programme is a quiz show called *In, Out*. I watch it ....
weekend. The .... are very clever. It's presented .... a university
professor.

2

| about | actors | interesting | operas |

I enjoy watching documentaries .... science. They are very ....
I rarely watch soap .... because I think the .... are terrible.

3

| always | exciting | series | stars |

I like watching a drama .... called *School Time*. I .... watch it
with my brother. It .... our favourite actor and it's a very ....
programme.

4

| contestants | funny | sometimes | talk |

I like .... shows. The guests are usually very .... I like game
shows too. The .... on game shows are .... really good.

Part 2: Skills development

Exam information

Part 2 tests your ability to talk without pausing and also your ability to plan and organize your answer.

1 Read the Part 2 task card below. Look at the underlined key words. Match the key words to the notes 1–5 below. There is one extra note.

Talk about a programme you learned something from.

You should say:

what type of programme it was
which were your favourite parts
who you watched it with

And explain what you learned from it.

1   interesting interviews with the writer's family and friends
2   learned about the writer's life, e.g. poor family, no qualifications, lived in different countries, now lives in her hometown.
3   documentary about a writer
4   watched it at college
5   with my classmates

2 Read the example answer below. Answer true or false for sentences 1–3.

I'd like to talk about a programme I learned something from. I learned about the writer's life. I learned she was from a poor family. I learned she had no qualifications from school. Then she lived in different countries. I learned that she now lives in her hometown and she writes there.

I watched it with my classmates. We watched it at college in a seminar. Then we talked about her life.

It was a documentary and it was about a famous writer. I enjoy reading her books. She writes about college students and their lives.

1 All the key words and notes are included. *True / False*
2 The answer follows the order on the task card. *True / False*
3 The answer is clear and easy to follow. *True / False*

Exam tip

Follow the order of the points on the task card. These organize your answer and help you to keep talking.

3　Read the example answer below. Answer true or false for sentences 1–3.

I'd like to talk about a programme I learned something from.

The programme was a very interesting documentary and it was about a famous writer. I enjoy watching this documentary series. It always has really interesting people or topics.

Firstly, I liked everything in the documentary, but my favourite parts were the interviews with her family and friends. A good example of this is the interview with her sister. She talked about their life when they were young children. She was very funny. There was one old friend from the writer's school and they are still friends today. I liked learning about the writer's personal life.

I watched it with my classmates. We watched it at college in a seminar. It was part of the course and then we gave a presentation about her life.

I learned lots of things from the documentary. For example, I learned she was from a poor family. I learned she had no qualifications from school and then she lived in different countries. Finally, I learned that she now lives in her hometown and she writes there.

1　All the key words and notes are included. *True / False*
2　The answer follows the order on the task card. *True / False*
3　The answer is clear and easy to follow. *True / False*

4　Read the example answer in Exercise 3 again. Find and underline two phrases for giving examples and two phrases for organizing your answers.

5　Look back at the task card in Exercise 1. Plan your answer. Follow the points below:

- Make notes on each key word.
- Write sentences using your notes.
- Include the underlined phrases from Exercise 3.

6　Record your answer. Use your notes to help you.

7　Listen to your answer. Can you improve it? Try to give your answer again. Refer to the task card in Exercise 1 but do not use your notes this time.

Exam tip

Remember there are different topics and different task cards in each IELTS exam. Do not memorise a speech on a topic for the exam.

Part 3: Exam practice

Part 1

1 Read the Part 1 questions. Record your answer to each question.

> When did you last watch television?
>
> What do you usually watch on television?
>
> What are some popular programmes in your country?
>
> Why do you think some TV programmes are popular?

Part 2

2 Read the Part 2 task card. Plan your answer. You have one minute for this in the exam. Then record your answer. You have one to two minutes for this in the exam.

> **Talk about a TV programme you enjoy watching.**
>
> You should say:
>
> **what type of programme it is**
> **which are your favourite parts**
> **when and where you watch it**
>
> And explain why you enjoy watching it.

Exam tip

Remember to use phrases for expressing preferences. See page 15.

Progress check

3 Listen to your answers. Tick the boxes below to assess your answers.

Do you …
include all the key words in your notes? ☐
follow the order on the task card? ☐
give an answer that is clear and easy to follow? ☐
include phrases to organize your answer? ☐
use vocabulary for describing types of programme? ☐
use adverbs of frequency? ☐
use phrases for expressing preferences? ☐

6 Weather

Part 1: Language development

Vocabulary: The weather

A   B   C   D

1 Match two words with each picture A–D above.

> cold   hot   rainy   snowy   stormy   sunny   wet   windy

2 Use your answers from Exercise 1 to complete the descriptions below.

Picture A   In my country, the monsoon season is from September to November. It's very
.... and ....

Picture B   In my country winter lasts from December to February. It's ....
and ....

Picture C   We often have thunderstorms in March or April in my country. It's ....
and ....

Picture D   The dry season lasts from May until October in my country. It's ....
and ....

3 Complete the table below with information about the seasons in your country.

season	Months	weather
autumn	*October and November*	*cold and windy*
dry season		
rainy season		
spring		
summer		
winter		

Vocabulary: Talking about the weather

4 Complete the sentences with the words and phrases in the box.

> favourite   it's   lasts   makes   really like   There's

1 My .... season is summer.
2 .... lots of rain during the monsoon season.
3 In winter, ... wet and stormy in my country.
4 Hot weather .... me feel really happy.
5 Winter .... for two months.
6 I .... stormy weather because it's exciting.

Watch Out!

It's + adjective = It's rainy/snowy/windy.
There's/There are + noun = *There's lots* of rain/snow/wind.

5 Complete the sentences below with your own ideas.

1 My favourites season is ...
2 In summer, it's ...
3 There's lots of rain/sun during ...

4 Summer / The dry season lasts for ...
5 Cold weather makes me feel ...
6 I really like ...

Pronunciation: Vowel sounds

6 🔊 25 Listen to the vowel sounds and the words, and repeat them.

uː	aʊ	ʌ	eɪ	ɔː	əʊ
monsoon	now	summer	favourite	stormy	cold

7 🔊 26 Listen to the words below and add them to the correct vowel sound in the table. Use a dictionary to check the meaning of the words.

> April   autumn   drought   humid   June   month
> November   outside   rainy   snowy   stormy   sunny

8 🔊 27 Listen and check. Then listen again and repeat the vowel sounds and the words.

Grammar: *Can / can't*

🔊 **9** **Listen and complete the sentences with *can* or *can't*.**
28

1 You .... go to the beach in the summer.

2 You .... do anything when the weather is very hot.

3 You .... play tennis outside when it's rainy.

4 The rainy season .... last for weeks.

5 You .... go skiing in hot and dry climates.

6 The weather .... change quickly in the mountains.

10 **Read the rules about *can* and *can't*. Then complete the sentences with your own ideas.**

• We use *can* to say that it is possible to do something.

• We use *can't* to say that it is not possible to do something.

• Put *can* or *can't* before the main verb.

• The form of the main verb doesn't change.

1 When it's sunny, you can ...

2 In cold weather you can't ...

3 In summer, you can ...

4 In the rainy season, you can't ...

11 **Complete the sentences with the words below. There is one extra word in each set.**

1

can	it's	makes	season	weather

My favourite .... is summer. I really like the summer because ....
always hot and sunny. You .... do lots of sports or you can sunbathe and relax
with friends. The hot weather always .... me feel happy and cheerful. I think
everybody likes the hot weather.

2

can't	drought	dry	for	monsoon

A .... means lots of rainy weather! In my country, this season
lasts .... about three or four months. It's boring and you ....
do anything outside. It's humid and I don't like it. I prefer the .... weather
because I like being outside.

3

can	from	stormy	there's	thunderstorms

In my country, it's very cold in winter. .... lots of snow and you ....
go skiing or visit the mountains. This is my favourite season. It lasts ....
November to February. It's different from summer because summer lasts for about six
months. It's really hot and dry and there are .... at night.

Part 2: Skills development

Exam information

Part 1 tests your ability to understand general questions and to give relevant answers. It also tests your ability to expand your answers.

Part 2 tests your ability to give a fluent and organized answer. It also tests your ability to include extra information using relevant language.

Part 1

1 Read the Part 1 questions and answers below. Choose the correct answer (a or b).

1 How many seasons does your country have?
   a My country has four seasons.
   b There are many seasons in my country.

2 What's your favourite season of the year?
   a Hot and sunny. This is my favourite weather.
   b Summer. This is my favourite season.

3 How do rainy days make you feel?
   a I feel very sad on rainy days.
   b Yes, rainy days make you feel.

4 What do you like doing when it's hot?
   a I like it when it's hot, yes.
   b I like going to the beach.

🔊 **2** Listen and check.
29

Exam tip

Listen carefully to the question and give a relevant answer. Then expand your answer, for example give a reason or an explanation.

3 Read the correct answers again. Can you make the answers longer? Add a sentence to each correct answer in Exercise 1.

   1 I like it because the weather is hot and sunny.
   2 The seasons are spring, summer, autumn and winter.
   3 You can go swimming or you can meet friends there.
   4 You can't go outside and do any sports.

4 Answer each question in Exercise 1. Include a reason or an explanation in each answer.

Part 2

5 Read the task card and the example answer. What is the problem with the example answer?

    a It includes lots of extra information.

    b It doesn't include extra information.

> **Describe your favourite type of weather.**
>
> You should say:
>
> **what the type of weather is**
> **how often you experience this type of weather**
> **what you like doing in this weather**
>
> And explain why it is your favourite type of weather.

I'd like to describe my favourite type of weather. My country has three seasons and there are lots of types of weather. (1) ....

Yes, wet weather is my favourite. I like going shopping when the weather is wet because the shops are all indoors. (2) ....

I often experience this weather in other countries. I like travelling in Europe and I always take my umbrella with me. The wet weather lasts for a long time there. (3) ....

This weather is good for relaxing. For example, you can stay at home and just watch television. (4) ....

6 Read the sentences below. These all add extra information to the example answer in Exercise 5. Read the example answer again and add a sentence to the end of each paragraph.

    a You can chat to your friends online too.

    b It is different from my country because the rainy season only lasts for two months.

    c I also like cooking delicious meals for my family when there's lots of rain.

    d It is a difficult choice for me, but I think my favourite is wet weather.

7 Add two more sentences to expand the example answer in Exercise 5. Choose where to add the extra information. Then practise saying the answer.

8 Read the task card in Exercise 5 again. Plan your own answer. Remember to add extra information to each part of your answer.

9 Record your answer.

Part 3: Exam practice

Part 1

1 **Read the Part 1 questions. Record your answer to each question.**

    1 How many seasons does your country have?

    2 What's the weather like in your country?

    3 How do rainy days make you feel?

    4 What do you like doing when it's hot?

Part 2

2 **Read the Part 2 task card. Plan your answer. You have one minute for this in the exam. Then record your answer. You have one to two minutes for this in the exam.**

> **Describe your favourite season in your country.**
>
> You should say:
>
> **when that season is from and to**
> **what the weather is like**
> **how it is different from other seasons in your country**
>
> And explain why it is your favourite season.

Exam tip

You can also use vocabulary for free time activities when you talk about the weather.
See page 14.

Progress check

3 **Listen to your answers. Tick the boxes below to assess your answers.**

Do you …
give a relevant answer and expand your answer in Part 1? ☐
add extra information to your answer in Part 2? ☐
use vocabulary for talking about the weather? ☐
use vocabulary for free time activities? ☐
pronounce vowel sounds correctly? ☐
use *can / can't* correctly? ☐

Review 2

1 Find **12** places in cities below.

gallerybeachbridgecaféfactoryharbourhotelparkriverstadiumtheatreskyscraper

2 Match 1–5 to a–e to make descriptions of a city.

1 It's a
2 It's near the
3 It's got
4 It is famous for
5 I really like it because

a the people are very friendly.
b lots of accommodation for tourists.
c airport.
d modern city.
e its university.

3 Write sentences with *There is, There isn't, There are* or *There aren't*.

1 ✓ a harbour   *There is a harbour.*
2 ✓ lots of people   ....
3 ✗ much traffic   ....
4 ✗ any markets   ....
5 ✓ two museums   ....
6 ✗ a beach   ....
7 ✗ any shopping malls   ....
8 ✓ a football stadium   ....

4 Add the words to the table.

actors   characters   contestants   documentary   game show   guests   news
participants   presenter   reality TV show   soap opera   talk show

types of people	types of programme

5 Complete the descriptions of programmes with the words in the box below.

> about   best   good   presented   set   stars

1 It's .... a school.
2 It's .... in Australia.
3 It's .... by different people every week.
4 It .... lots of great actors.
5 It's .... entertainment.
6 The thing I like .... is the exciting plots.

6 Read the table which shows how often Matteo watches TV programmes. Write sentences with an adverb of frequency.

100%	sports programmes	Matteo always watches sport programmes.
80%	documentaries	(1)
60%	chat shows	Matteo often watches chat shows.
40%	dramas	(2)
10%	reality TV shows	(3)
0%	soap operas	(4)

7 Find four pairs of opposite words about the weather in the box.

> cold   drought   dry   hot   monsoon   rainy   sunny   wet

8 Choose the correct option for talking about the weather.

1 My favourite *season / weather* is summer.
2 Winter lasts *for / from* four months.
3 In spring, it's *rain / rainy*.
4 Cold weather makes me *like / feel* sad.
5 In my country, we often *have / it's* storms.

9 Complete the sentences with *can* or *can't*.

1 In cold weather, you .... go to the beach.
2 You .... go to the gym when it's rainy or when it's sunny.
3 The dry season .... last for months in my country.
4 In the rainy season, you .... go outside because it's very wet.
5 You .... go skiing when it's snowy.
6 You .... play tennis outside when it's windy.

7 Studying

AIMS: Talking about studying • Using collocations • Pronunciation: Word stress • Present continuous
• Skills development: Using a range of vocabulary • Exam practice: Part 1, Part 2, and Part 3

Part 1: Language development

Vocabulary: Academic subjects

 A    B    C    D

1   Match four of the subjects below to the pictures above. Use your dictionary to help you.

> art   business studies   computer science   engineering
> history   law   linguistics   literature   mathematics   medicine

2   Listen to three students talking about their course. Complete each description with the words below. Then listen again and check.

30

> course   difficult   director   doctor   interesting
> law   lawyer   lectures   medicine

1   I'm studying .... It's hard work and there are lots of ....,
    but I enjoy helping people. I'm in my first year and I'd like to be a ....

2   I'm doing a business studies .... It's about the different parts of a
    business, like finance, people, or marketing. It's really .... I'd like to
    be a company ....

3   I'm studying .... It's about the legal system in different countries. I
    think it's a very .... course and there are lots of deadlines. I'd like to be
    a ....

Watch Out!

I'm **studying** medicine.
I'm **learning about** health and illness.

Pronunciation: Word stress

3 How many syllables are in these words?

business ....   mathematics ....

literature ....   university ....

4 Listen and check. Then listen again and add the words to the correct stress patterns in the table below.

31

1 [O o]	2 [O o o]	3 [o o O o]	4 [o o O o o]

5 Listen to the words below and add them to the table in Exercise 4.

32

chemistry   college   deadline   engineering   graduate   graduation

history   lecture   medicine   presentation   project   timetable

6 Listen and check your answers to Exercises 4 and 5. Listen again and repeat the words.

33

Vocabulary: Collocations

7 Match the verbs 1–5 with the nouns a–e to make collocations about studying. Then match the verbs 6–10 with the nouns f–j to make more collocations.

1	apply	**a**	presentations
2	be	**b**	for a scholarship
3	do	**c**	good results
4	get	**d**	my homework
5	give	**e**	in my first/second/final year

6	go	**f**	in halls / with my family
7	graduate	**g**	extra tuition
8	have	**h**	to lectures / college
9	live	**i**	an essay
10	write	**j**	from university

8 Complete the sentences below with nouns from Exercise 7.

1 I hope I get good .... this semester.
2 I graduated from .... last summer.
3 I'm in my final .... at university.
4 I don't like giving ....
5 I'm writing an .... on international finance.

Grammar: Present continuous

🔊 **9** Listen to the three speakers. Complete the sentences with the correct names: Lara, Dee or
34 Marcel.

a .... is filling out an application form.
b .... is having extra tuition.
c .... is preparing a presentation.

10 Look at the table and complete the rule.

• Use the present continuous to talk about an activity happening *in the past* / *now*.

I	'm	'm not	
He / She / It	's	's not	studying English this semester.
You / We / They	're	're not	

🔊 **11** Listen to the speakers again and read the texts below. Underline the twelve examples of the
34 present continuous.

1 I'm revising for an exam. It's my final year and I'm working very hard. I'm having extra tuition and my grades are improving.

2 I'm visiting my brother at college. He's living in halls this year and he's having a great time. I'm helping him with his coursework this semester and we're preparing a presentation at the moment.

3 I'm thinking about doing another course next year. I'm applying for a scholarship at a university in my hometown and I'm filling out the application form now.

12 Complete the sentences below to describe what you are doing.

1 At the moment, I'm …
2 This semester I'm …

Watch Out!

at the moment = now or the next two/three days

Part 2: Skills development

Exam information

In Part 2, you talk for one to two minutes about the task card. Then the examiner asks you one or two questions related to your answer and this completes Part 2. These questions test your ability to give a relevant answer with a range of vocabulary.

Part 2

1 🔊 35 Imagine you have completed your two-minute talk on the Part 2 task card below. The examiner will ask you one more question to complete Part 2. Listen to an example answer. Which question (1 or 2) does it answer?

> **Talk about a subject you are studying.**
>
> You should say:
>
> **what subject you are studying**
> **what the subject is about**
> **how you feel about it**
>
> And explain why you are interested in it.

    1 Would you like a job connected to the subject you are studying?

    2 Are your friends or family interested in the subject too?

2 🔊 35 Read and listen to the example answer again. Write T (true) or F (false) for sentences 1–3 below.

Yes, yes they are. My father and my brother studied law at university, and they think it is a very nice subject. My mother thinks it is nice and always asks me questions about law. I have lots of friends on the course, and we want to get a nice job when we graduate.

    1 The answer is relevant to the topic. ....

    2 The answer includes all parts of the question. ....

    3 The speaker repeats some words. ....

3 Look at the example answer in Exercise 2 again. Underline the three adjectives. Replace each adjective with one of the adjectives below.

    good   important   interesting

4 🔊 36 Listen and check. Assess the answer again using sentences 1–3 in Exercise 2. Which answer has changed?

Exam tip

Use a range of adjectives (*good, important, interesting*). Try not to repeat words.

5 Record your answers to the questions in Exercise 1.

6 Listen to your answers and assess them.

- Are your answers relevant to the topic?
- Do you answer all parts of the question?
- Do you repeat any words?
- How many different adjectives did you use?

Part 3

Exam information

Part 3 tests your ability to express your opinion in a clear way and to use relevant language and a range of vocabulary.

🔊 **7**
37

Read the three questions below. Then listen to three people answering the questions. Match each question a–c to a speaker 1–3.

   a Is it a good idea to live with your family when you are studying? ....

   b Compare your experience of education to your parents' generation. ....

   c Do you think your country has a good education system? ....

8 Look at three adverbs from the answers in Exercise 7. Match them to the correct meaning.

   1 definitely   **a** I'm pleased about this.

   2 fortunately   **b** I'm not happy about this.

   3 unfortunately   **c** I agree completely.

Exam tip

Using adverbs shows the examiner you can express your opinion in different ways.

9 Look at the Part 3 questions in Exercise 7 again. Think about your answers and how you will express your opinions. Which adverbs will you use?

10 Record your answers. Then listen to your answers and assess each one. Choose T (true) or F (false) for the points below.

   1 The answer is four or more sentences long. *T | F*

   2 The answer is relevant to the topic. *T | F*

   3 The answer includes a range of adjectives and adverbs. *T | F*

11 For extra practice, go to page 25 and answer the Part 3 questions again. Try to use a range of vocabulary in your answers.

Part 3: Exam practice

Part 1

🔊 **1** Listen to five Part 1 questions. Record your answer to each question.
38

Part 2

2 Read the Part 2 task card. Plan your answer. You have one minute for this in the exam. Then record your answer. You have one to two minutes for this in the exam.

> **Talk about a subject you are studying.**
>
> You should say:
>
> **which subject you are studying**
>
> **what the subject is about**
>
> **how you feel about it**
>
> And explain why you are interested in it.

3 Answer the question below to complete Part 2. Record your answer.

Would you like a job related to this subject?

Part 3

🔊 **4** Listen to five Part 3 questions. Answer two of the questions and record your answer.
39

> ## Exam tip
> Remember to include other relevant grammar like the past simple and the present simple.

Progress check

5 Listen to your answers. Tick the boxes below to assess your answers.

Do you …
answer all parts of the task in Part 2? ☐
use a range of adjectives and adverbs in your answers? ☐
give an answer four or more sentences long in Part 3? ☐
use vocabulary and collocations for talking about studying? ☐
use study and learn correctly? ☐
use the correct word stress? ☐
use the present continuous? ☐

8 Work

AIMS: Talking about jobs • Describing your job • *Have to* • Skills development: Useful phrases
• Exam practice: Part 1, Part 2, and Part 3

Part 1: Language development

Vocabulary: Jobs

  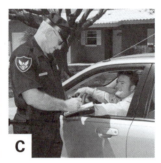 

A   B   C   D

1 **Which jobs can you see in the photos? Match four of the jobs below with the photos above.**

> businessman   chef   journalist   lawyer   nurse
> police officer   personal assistant   teacher   volunteer

2 **Complete the descriptions below with the jobs from Exercise 1. Use your dictionary to help you.**

    1 I'm a .... and I work different shifts each week. My job is to keep people safe.

    2 I work for a national newspaper. I interview people and write articles. I'm a ....

    3 I help my patients every day. I work in a hospital and I'm a ....

    4 I work as a .... I work with animals and I have to look after them every day. I don't get paid for my work.

    5 I'm a .... and I work in the city. I work with different companies and I make lots of money.

    6 I work in a school and my job is to help students pass exams. I'm a ....

 3 **Listen and check.**
40

4 What do you do? Write a short description of a job you have now or had in the past.

> *Watch Out!*
>
> **Learn the correct prepositions.**
>
> I work **in** a hospital / the city / a school. I work **with** animals / different companies.
> I work **for** a national newspaper.

Vocabulary: Your job

5 Read the different reasons for applying for a job below. In your opinion, which ones are important to you for your next job?

to earn a good salary	to work flexible hours
to help people	to work for a well-known company
to travel the world	to work in a modern office
to use languages	to work with different people

🔊 6 Listen to three people talking about how they got a job. Which speaker (a, b or c)
41

1 wrote to the company director? ....   3 worked during the summer? ....
2 had a part-time job? ....   4 worked as a volunteer? ....

7 Listen to the three speakers again. Choose the correct options below.

a I had a *part-time / temporary* job at the company and I really enjoyed it. My boss and my colleagues were professional but very friendly. I *volunteered / applied* for a full-time job in my final year at university and I got it. The job is well-paid so I'm *earning / saving* a good salary and I also travel to lots of different countries. It's an exciting job.

b I work as a personal assistant at a very well-known *company / office*. I love my job. I got my job last year. I worked here as a volunteer to get *work experience / a qualification*. I really enjoyed it, so I wrote to the company director and asked for a job. I *use my languages / travel the world* regularly and I work *with different people / flexible hours*.

c Two years ago, I worked as a volunteer in a hospital because I wanted to *help people / work with different people*. I went to university, but I worked at the hospital each summer. I didn't want to *travel the world / work in a modern office*, so I applied for the job. Now I'm *working flexible hours / earning a good salary* and it's my dream job!

> *Watch Out!*
>
> My brother has two **jobs**. He works in a café and he works a fitness instructor. = specific jobs
>
> It's difficult for people to find **work** in my country. = general description

8 Think about a job you applied for in the past. Write a short description. Include answers to these questions.

- What was the job?
- Where was it?
- Was it a full-time or part-time job?
- Why did you apply for this job?

Grammar: *Have to*

9 Read the rule and look at the table. Then read the interview below and complete the gaps with the correct form of *have to*.

- *Have to* = there is an obligation or requirement to do something.

I / We / You / They	(present) have to	don't have to	work long hours.
	(past) had to	didn't have to	get a qualification.
He / She / It	(present) has to	doesn't have to	
	(past) had to	didn't have to	

A: What do you do?

B: I'm a manager. I work for a well-known international company, so I often (1) .... travel to different offices around the world.

A: Did you have to get any qualifications or do any training for your job?

B: Yes, I did. I (2) .... complete three training courses. Thankfully, I (3) .... revise for any exams because the assessment was an interview and giving a presentation.

A: Do you have to wear a uniform or smart clothes?

B: I (4) .... wear a uniform, but I (5) .... wear a suit to meetings.

A: Do you have to work long hours?

B: Yes. At the moment, I need to work hard to complete a project.

A: What does your job involve?

B: Well, I (6) .... meet lots of people, but I (7) .... speak different languages because we all speak English. I often (8) .... prepare reports or give presentations.

◀)) 10 Listen and check.
42

11 Answer the interview questions in Exercise 9 about your job.

12 Complete the text with the words below. There is one extra word.

> as   for   salary   to   use   well-known   well-paid

I really like my job. I work (1) .... a part-time manager in a university. I applied for the job last year and then I had (2) .... go for an interview with the manager. We talked about my work experience and why I wanted to work (3) .... the university. The university department is very (4) .... all over the world and I wanted to (5) .... my languages and meet new people. My job isn't (6) .... but I don't have to worry about money because I live with my family.

Part 2: Skills development

Exam information

The Speaking test assesses your ability to speak coherently (to give answers that are easy to follow and understand) and fluently (to keep talking without repeating words and without pauses).

Part 3

1 **Read the Part 3 questions below and underline the key words.**

    1 Compare your experience of finding a job to your parents' generation.

    2 Many people think that work experience is the best way to learn about a job. What is your point of view?

    3 In your opinion, do people work more now than in the past?

    4 Do you think companies need people to travel to an office and work there, or can people work from home?

2 **Read the Part 3 questions again. What are the questions asking you to do?**

    a to give your opinion on an issue

    b to compare the past to the present

3 **Read the example answer below. Which question from Exercise 1 is it answering?**

> **That's an (1)** .... **question. Let me (2)** .... I definitely think that work experience is an important way to learn about a job. I studied business for three years and I graduated with honours. Then I got a good job, but it was really hard work and tiring. **I (3)** .... **that** your first job is always difficult. I learnt lots in my first year there. But my course did help me, for example I understood lots of basic points about business and finance. **There are pros and (4)** ....Work experience is an excellent way to learn about a job in real life, but education or training gives you time to learn the theories.

🔊 **4** **43** **Look at the bold phrases in Exercise 3. Listen to the example answer and complete the gaps in the phrases. How do the useful phrases help the speaker and improve the answer?**

Exam tip

Including useful phrases in your answers gives you time to think and relax in the test. It also shows the examiner you are speaking at a natural pace and without pauses.

5 Listen to another example answer. Which question from Exercise 1 does it answer?

6 Listen again and complete the useful phrases below.

    1 That's ....
    2 Let me ....
    3 I .... that ...
    4 I'm not ....
    5 There are advantages and ....

7 Look back at question 2 in Exercise 1. Think about your answer and which relevant useful phrases you can include. Record your answer.

8 Listen to your answer. Does your answer sound natural? Practise saying your answer again and sounding natural. Then record your answer again.

> ## Exam tip
>
> In Part 3, you can ask the examiner to repeat the question if you don't understand or if you don't hear. Say: *Can you repeat the question, please?*

9 Listen to two Part 3 questions. Then answer the questions below.

    a Do you have to give your opinion on an issue or to compare the past to the present?
    b Which useful phrases can you include?

10 Close your book. Listen to the two Part 3 questions again. Record your answers.

11 Listen to your answers. Answer the questions below.

    1 Do the answers sound natural?
    2 How many pauses are there?
    3 How many useful phrases are there?

12 Practise saying your answers again to improve your performance. Record your answers again.

Part 3: Exam practice

Part 1

1   Read the Part 1 questions. Record your answer to each question.

  1   What do you do?
  2   Do you enjoy your work? Why? Why not?
  3   Is there another type of work you would like to do?
  4   Describe the company or organization you work for.
  5   Describe a typical day in your job.

Part 2

2   Read the Part 2 task card. Plan your answer. You have one minute for this in the exam. Then record your answer. You have one to two minutes for this in the exam.

> Describe a job you have now or had in the past. You should say:
>
> **how you got the job**
> **what the job involves**
> **why you wanted the job**
>
> And describe how well you do or did the job.

3   Answer the question below to complete Part 2. Record your answer.

  What are / were your colleagues like?

Part 3

4   Read the Part 3 questions. Answer two of the questions and record your answer.

  1   In your opinion, is it a good idea for families to work together?
  2   Many people think that work experience is the best way to learn about a job. What is your point of view?
  3   In your opinion, do people work more now than in the past?
  4   Do you think working from home is a good idea?

Progress check

5   Listen to your answers. Tick the boxes below to assess your answers.

  Do you …
  answer the Part 3 questions by speculating or comparing?
  include useful phrases in Part 3 to give you time to think?
  speak at a natural speed without pauses?
  use vocabulary for talking about your job?
  use the correct propositions with work?
  use have to to talk about an obligation?

9 Holidays and travel

AIMS: Talking about holidays • Using adjectives in descriptions • *Be going* to • Pronunciation: /ə/ and sentence stress • Skills development: Using a range of vocabulary • Exam practice: Part 1, Part 2, and Part 3

Part 1: Language development

Vocabulary: Holidays

A   B   C   D

1 Match the photos to four types of holidays below. Use your dictionary to help you.

> activity holiday   beach holiday   city break   coach tour   cruise
> family holiday   honeymoon   learning holiday   round-the-world trip   safari

2 Put the words in the box with the correct verb in the table below.

> day trips   historical sites   lessons or a course   local festivals
> new sports   photos   sightseeing   swimming in the sea
> tourist attractions   traditional restaurants   water sports

do	
eat in	
go	
go on	
learn	
take	
visit	
watch	

3 Write a short description of your last holiday. Use the expressions from Exercise 2 to describe what you did.

Vocabulary: Opposite adjectives

4 Match the adjectives 1–6 to their opposites a–f.

1 beautiful		**a**	traditional
2 comfortable		**b**	unfriendly
3 delicious		**c**	boring
4 exciting		**d**	horrible
5 friendly		**e**	disgusting
6 modern		**f**	uncomfortable

5 Complete the sentences with a suitable adjective from Exercise 4.

1 The beaches were .... and the weather was lovely!

2 We stayed in a .... hotel, it was lovely!

3 I learnt water sports. It was .... and I'd like to do it again.

4 We went on a family holiday last year and my mother cooked .... meals.

5 I went on a city break to New York City and the people were so ....

6 My sister and I did an English course abroad and the teachers were very ....

7 There was a short bus ride to the hotel, but the journey was really ....

Grammar: Future: *Be going to*

🔊 **6** Listen to Richard talking about his holiday plans. Which activities is he going to do?
46 Put a ✓ or a ✗ in the table.

	Richard	my last holiday	my next holiday
1 learn new sports			
2 take lessons			
3 go swimming in the sea			
4 go sightseeing			
5 visit local festivals			
6 eat in traditional restaurants			
7 go on day trips			

7 Look at the activities in Exercise 8 again and complete the table with your own answers. Put a ✓ or a ✗ for activities you did on your last holiday and activities you're going to do on your next holiday.

8 Read the rule and look at the table below. Then look at your answers to Exercise 7 and describe what you're going to do on your next holiday.

- Use *be going to* + an infinitive.
- Use *be going to* for future plans.

I	'm / am	'm not / am not	going to take lots of photos.
He / She / It	's / is	isn't / is not	
We / You / They	're / are	aren't / are not	going to visit Europe next year.

Watch Out!

I'd like to travel the world. = a hope for the future

I'm going to visit Europe next year. = a plan or decision about the future

Pronunciation: /ə/ and sentence stress

◄)) **9** Listen to the two sentences below. How is *to* pronounced – strong (with stress) /tuː/ or
47 weak (no stress) /tə/?

    1 I'm going **to** study in America.   **2** I'm going **to** study in America.

◄)) **10** Read and listen to the sentences below. Pay attention to the underlined stressed words. The
48 listen again and repeat each sentence.

    1 I'm <u>going</u> to <u>visit</u> <u>England</u>.   **2** I'm <u>not going</u> to <u>visit</u> <u>Spain</u>.

◄)) **11** Listen to the sentences below. Underline the stressed words.
49

    1 I'm going to stay in a hotel.
    2 I'm not going to take any photos.
    3 I'm going to eat in traditional restaurants.
    4 We're going to visit historical sites.
    5 We're not going to learn a new sport.
    6 We're going to go sightseeing.

◄)) **12** Listen again to the sentences in Exercise 11 and repeat. Practise using the /ə/ sound and
49 using correct sentence stress.

Exam tip

/ə/ is a very common and important sound in English. Practise using /ə/ to improve your English pronunciation.

Part 2: Skills development

Exam information

The Speaking test assesses your ability to use a range of relevant vocabulary to talk about the different IELTS topics.

Part 1

1 Match the topics 1–8 to the groups of words a–h.

1	Family	**a**	characters, dramatic, plots, series, soap operas
2	Free time activities	**b**	accommodation, busy, gallery, skyscraper, traditional food
3	Special occasions	**c**	colleague, office, part-time, salary, volunteer
4	Cities	**d**	business studies, grades, literature, medicine, university
5	TV and radio programmes	**e**	boring, chatting online, doing nothing, meeting friends, prefer
6	The weather	**f**	costume, dance, make, parade, presents
7	Studying	**g**	bossy, funny, husband, look like, parents
8	Work	**h**	autumn, monsoon, November, season, snowy

2 Look at the topics in Exercise 1 again. Choose three topics. Can you say all the words correctly? Can you use each word in a sentence? If not, go back to the relevant unit and revise the vocabulary.

Exam tip

Revise your vocabulary regularly and practise using it. This helps you to remember your vocabulary in the test and to use your vocabulary with the correct topics.

3 Use the topics in Exercise 1 to answer the Part 1 questions below. Record your answers.

1 Do you have a large family?

2 How often do you read newspapers?

3 Do you enjoy going to special occasions?

4 Where is your hometown located?

5 What do you usually watch on television?

6 What's the weather like in your country?

7 What are you studying now?

8 What do you do?

4 Listen to your answers. Go to the glossary on page 129 and tick the words you used. Could you use more words? Answer the questions again and try to use more words.

Part 2

5 Read the Part 2 task card below. Think and plan your answer. Which words and phrases can you include to show your range of vocabulary? Which useful phrases can you include to organize your answer?

> **Describe a friend that you like spending time with.**
>
> You should say:
>
> **when and how you met**
> **how often you see this friend**
> **what kind of personality your friend has**
>
> And say why you like spending time with this friend.

6 Record your answer. Then listen to your answer. Could you include more vocabulary and more useful phrases? Record your answer again and try to improve it.

🔊 **7** Listen to a question related to the task card in Exercise 5. Record your answer.
50

Part 3

🔊 **8** Listen to four Part 3 questions. What is each question asking you to do? Write O (give your
51   opinion) or C (compare the past to the present).

1 ....   2 ....   3 ....   4 ....

9 Which useful phrases below could you include in your answers? Can you think of other useful phrases?

> I'm not sure.   Let me see.   That's interesting.   There are pros and cons.

🔊 **10** Listen to the Part 3 questions in Exercise 8 again. Record your answers.
51

11 Listen to your answers. Could you include more vocabulary and more useful phrases? Record your answer again and try to improve it.

Part 3: Exam practice

Part 1

🔊 **1** Listen to five Part 1 questions. Record your answer to each question.
52

Part 2

2 Listen to and read the Part 2 task card below. Plan your answer. You have one minute for this in the exam. Then record your answer. You have one to two minutes for this in the exam.

> **Talk about a special holiday or trip.**
>
> You should say:
>
> **what it was**
> **when and where you went**
> **what you did**
>
> And explain why it is special to you.

3 Answer the question below to complete Part 2. Record your answer.

Are you going to go on a similar trip in the future?

Part 3

🔊 **4** Listen to four Part 3 questions. Answer the questions and record your answer.
53

Progress check

5 Listen to your answers. Tick the boxes below to assess your answers.

Do you …
include a range of vocabulary in all your answers? ☐
understand Part 3 questions and compare/give your opinion? ☐
use vocabulary for talking about holidays? ☐
use adjectives to improve your descriptions? ☐
use *be going to* to talk about future plans? ☐
pronounce /ə/ correctly and use correct sentence stress? ☐

Review 3

1   Write the academic subject in which you learn about the things below.

    1   calculations and formulas   *m* ....

    2   designing and building   *e* ....

    3   drugs and treatment   *m* ....

    4   how computers work   *c* .... *s* ....

    5   important events in the past   *h* ....

    6   the legal system   *l* ....

2   Choose the correct verb to complete the collocations about studying.

    1   I'm *applying / writing* for a scholarship for university.

    2   I feel very nervous before *giving / saying* presentations.

    3   It's important to *get / write* good results in tests.

    4   I *had / went* extra tuition in my final year.

    5   I *graduated / passed* from university in June.

    6   I prefer *applying / writing* essays to exams.

3   Complete the sentences with the correct present continuous form of the verb in brackets.

    1   I .... my best friend at college. *(visit)*

    2   I .... about studying overseas. *(think)*

    3   My grades .... this semester. *(improve)*

    4   I .... hard because I want to pass my exams. *(work)*

    5   We .... a presentation for my tutor. *(prepare)*

    6   I .... about different cultures and languages. *(learn)*

4   Match the statements 1–8 with the jobs below.

> businessman   chef   journalist   lawyer   nurse   police officer   teacher   volunteer

    1   I write articles for newspapers.

    2   I don't get a salary.

    3   I catch criminals.

    4   I help companies make money.

    5   I work in a hospital with doctors.

    6   I use the legal system to help people.

    7   I work in a classroom.

    8   I cook lots of different food.

5 **Choose the correct word in the descriptions of work below.**

1 I think it's important to *earn / save* a good salary.
2 I had a temporary *job / work* in the summer.
3 I'd like to be a *volunteer / part-time* overseas.
4 Most people like working flexible *hours / time*.
5 I enjoy *talking / using* my languages in my job.
6 I did *career / work* experience before I got the job.

6 **Write sentences with the correct form of *have to* or *(don't) have to*.**

1 ✓ I .... work long hours in my job.
2 ✗ I .... wear a uniform.
3 ✓ I .... take a course last year.
4 ✓ My colleague and I .... prepare reports.
5 ✗ I .... give presentations.
6 ✓ In my job, you .... use your languages.

7 **Match the words to make places you visit or activities you do on holiday.**

1 historical   **a** restaurants
2 local   **b** sightseeing
3 go   **c** sites
4 tourist   **d** attractions
5 traditional   **e** sports
6 water   **f** festivals

8 **Find five pairs of opposite adjectives in the box.**

beautiful   boring   comfortable   exciting   friendly   horrible
modern   traditional   uncomfortable   unfriendly

9 **Listen and complete the sentences about Aftab's holiday plans with *I'm going* to or *I'm not going* to.**

54

1 .... learn new sports.
2 .... go swimming in the sea.
3 .... go sightseeing.
4 .... visit local festivals.
5 .... eat in traditional restaurants.
6 .... take lots of photos.

10 Health

Part 1: Language development

Vocabulary: healthy activities

 A  B  C  D

1 Match the activities below with the photos A–D.

> do sports   eat well   play board games   sleep for eight hours every night

---

Watch Out!

Use an adverb with a verb.   **Don't use an adjective with a verb.**

It's important to eat well.   ~~It's important to eat good.~~

---

2 Complete the table with the activities from Exercise 1 and the activities below.

> do tae kwon do   do yoga   draw pictures   have a healthy diet
> play a musical instrument   play brain training games   play table tennis

good for your mind	good for your body	good for both

🔊 **3**
55

Listen to Jack talking about things he does to keep healthy. Complete the description below.

> brain training games   doing yoga   good for   important to   makes me feel   on my own

I like (1) .... and playing (2) .... I enjoy doing these activities (3) .... because I work in a busy, noisy office every day. It's (4) .... relax after a hard day. Yoga (5) .... relaxed and I think brain training games are (6) .... my mind.

4   Write a short description of something you do to keep healthy. Say:

- what it is
- how often you do it
- where you do it
- who you do it with

Vocabulary: Giving explanations

🔊 **5**
56

Listen to Charles and Rosa talking about healthy activities they do. What is the activity they like doing and who do they do it with?

🔊 **6**
56

Listen again and write the words in the box next to the correct sentence beginnings.

> happy   hard   keep your mind active

1 It's ....
2 It's important to ....
3 It makes me feel ....

7   Match the words and phrases below to the sentence beginnings in Exercise 6.

> challenging   great   healthy   interesting   keep fit
> relax after college   relaxed   relaxing   work in a team

8   Think of two healthy activities you do and give an explanation about why you like each one. Use the expressions in Exercises 6 and 7 to help you.

1 ....
....
2 ....
....

Pronunciation: Contractions

9 Circle the contraction (= two words made into one word) in each sentence.

    1 It's good for you.

    2 It isn't good for you.

    3 It's really bad for you.

    4 It's important to stay healthy.

    5 You shouldn't eat junk food.

 **10** Listen and repeat each sentence. Pay attention to the contractions.
57

> ## Exam tip
> Try to pronounce contractions clearly to make your speaking sound natural.

Grammar: *Should / shouldn't*

11 Read the rules. Then choose the correct words to complete the sentences.

- Use *should* or *shouldn't* to make a suggestion.
- Use *should* to say something is a good idea.
- Use *shouldn't to* say something is a bad idea.
- Put should and *shouldn't* before the main verb.

    1 I *should / shouldn't* eat lots of junk food. It isn't good for my body.

    2 I *should / shouldn't* try to do more exercise. It's important to stay healthy.

    3 Playing the piano makes me feel relaxed. You *should / shouldn't* try it.

    4 You *should / shouldn't* study late at night. It's really bad for your health.

    5 People *should / shouldn't* play board games, like chess. It's good for your mind.

    6 You *should / shouldn't* ask your friend to do your homework.

Part 2: Skills development

Exam information

Part 1 tests your ability to answer different questions about your life. Part 3 tests your ability to give your opinion on different topics.

Part 1

1 Read the Part 1 questions and answers below. For each question, choose the answer (a or b) which is relevant.

1 Do you enjoy watching sports?
   a Yes, I enjoy watching sports. I like watching football and golf.
   b Yes, I enjoy sports. I play football every week and I think doing sports is good for you.

2 Do you work or are you a student?
   a I'm a student and I'm studying English. I'm in my first year at university.
   b I started studying English when I was at school. It was my favourite subject.

3 When do you see your friends and family?
   a Every day. I'm living with my parents at the moment and I see my friends at college every day.
   b Every day. I'm living with my parents at the moment and I visit my grandparents every weekend.

4 What do you like doing in your free time?
   a I don't have lots of hobbies because I work long hours.
   b I like meeting my friends and relaxing. I really enjoy going to the cinema and going shopping.

2 Now read the questions in Exercise 1 again and record your answers.

3 Listen to your answers and assess them. Are your answers relevant to the question?

Exam tip

Remember to only talk about relevant points or information in your answer.

🔊 **4** Listen to three Part 3 questions. Are the questions asking you (a) to give your opinion on an
58 issue, (b) to compare the past to the present or (c) to make a suggestion?

> **1** ....
> **2** ....
> **3** ....

Exam tip

Pay attention to the examiner's questions. Understand the type of question you have to answer: opinion, comparison, or suggestion.

5 Read the three answers below. Match the answers with the questions 1–3 in Exercise 4.

a Definitely. I think relaxing is a very important part of being healthy. We are always busy. We're travelling to work or college, we're meeting friends, we're doing homework. So in my opinion, I think it's important to slow down and relax. It is good for our bodies and our minds.

b That's a difficult question. Let me see. Unfortunately, in my country, young people like playing computer games, and they usually like eating junk food. We should encourage them to play game outdoors. For example, they could go to the beach and do water sports. We should encourage them to learn about food and cook some healthy food with their families.

c That's interesting. I think it's important to play sports. There are lots of different sports now, and you can learn a new sport wherever you live. Sports people earn a good salary. I think it's a good job. I'd like to be a professional golfer. But there are some boring sports. For example, I don't like watching motor racing.

🔊 **6** Listen and check. Then read the answers again and complete the table below.
59

	Answer a	Answer b	Answer c
1 Is the answer relevant to the question?			
2 What is the opinion, comparison or suggestion?			

7 Listen to the questions in Exercise 4 again and record your answers.

8 Listen to your answers and assess each of your answers.

- Is your answer relevant to the question?
- What is your opinion, comparison and suggestion?

🔊 **9** Close your book and listen to three Part 3 questions. Decide what the question is asking for
60 (opinion, comparison or suggestion) and then give your answers.

Part 3: Exam practice

Part 1

🔊 **1** Listen to five Part 1 questions. Record your answer to each question.
61

Part 2

2 Read the Part 2 task card below. Plan your answer. You have one minute for this in the exam. Then record your answer. You have one to two minutes for this in the exam.

> **Describe an activity you like doing to keep healthy. You should say:**
>
> **what it is**
> **when and where you do it**
> **how it keeps you healthy**
>
> And explain why you like doing it.

Exam tip

Remember to use the Present simple to talk about things you like doing in your life.

3 Answer the questions below to complete Part 2. Record your answer.

   1 Do your family like doing this activity?
   2 Would you like to spend more time on this activity?

Part 3

🔊 **4** Listen to four Part 3 questions. Answer the questions and record your answers.
62

Progress check

5 Listen to your answers. Tick the boxes below to assess your answers.

Do you

include relevant points in your answer? ☐
recognise the different Part 3 questions? ☐
use vocabulary for talking about healthy activities? ☐
use vocabulary for giving explanations about why you like an activity? ☐
use *should* and *shouldn't* to make suggestions? ☐
pronounce contractions correctly? ☐

11 Important events

AIMS: Talking about important events • Describing feelings • Pronunciation: Giving emphasis • Comparing • Skills development: Using a range of grammar • Exam practice: Part 1, Part 2, and Part 3

Part 1: Language development

Vocabulary: important events

A   B   C   D

1   **Match the photos to the events below. There are two extra events.**

> coming of age   getting married   getting your first job   graduating from university
> travelling on your own for the first time   winning a sports competition

🔊 **2**   **Listen to John talking about one of the events in Exercise 1. Answer the questions below.**
63

     1   What was the event?

     2   Who was there?

     3   How did he feel?

3   **Have you experienced one of the events in Exercise 1 or a similar event? How did you feel? Make notes. Then write a short description and record your description.**

     •   What was the event?

     •   Who was there?

     •   How did you feel?

Watch Out!

Learn the endings of irregular verbs: *feel – felt*

How did he feel?

I felt very excited.

Vocabulary: Describing feelings

4 Put the pairs of adjectives below into the correct group.

> bored/boring   delighted   excited/exciting   relaxed/relaxing   satisfied/satisfying
> surprised/surprising   terrified/terrifying   tired/tiring

negative feelings	positive feelings

🔊 **5** Listen to Paul talking about an important event. Circle the adjectives from Exercise 4 that
64   you hear.

6 Complete the gaps with your answers from Exercise 5. Then listen again and check.

> I was very nervous before the national championships. I felt (1) .... ! We travelled
> to the city the night before and it was a long and (2) .... journey on the bus. We
> were all really (3) .... when we woke up the next day. Finally, our match started. I
> was (4) .... because some of the players on my team were very (5) .... The
> opposition were an excellent team and the match was (6) .... , but thankfully we
> won! We were all (7) .... and I think our manager was (8) .... with the result.
> It was a really (9) .... event for me.

Watch Out!

Use adjectives ending with **-ed** to describe your feelings. We were all tired.

Use adjectives ending with **-ing** to describe a thing or an event. The match was tiring.

Pronunciation: Giving emphasis

🔊 **7** Listen to the sentences. Which word has the most stress in each sentence?
65
  1 I was very bored at my brother's graduation.
  2 I feel really tired at the end of the week.
  3 I was very surprised when I passed all my exams.
  4 I felt really excited when I travelled on my own.

🔊 **8** Listen again and repeat. Remember to stress *really* and *very* to give emphasis.
65

Grammar: Comparing

🔊 **9** **66** Listen to Peter comparing different events a student experiences. Match the sentence halves below. Then listen again and check.

1 I think the most important event	**a** undergraduates.
2 It is more important than	**b** taking exams.
3 Graduates are happier than	**c** for a student is graduation day.
4 Finding a job is more worrying than	**d** end-of-year exams.

10 Choose the correct word in each sentence.

1 It was the *more / most* exciting day of my life.

2 I think graduation day is a *more / most* important day than your first day at school.

3 In my opinion, studying in your hometown is *better than / best* studying in another town.

4 I really like travelling with friends. It's *more / most* interesting than travelling alone.

5 My *more / most* important event at university was passing my end-of-year exams.

6 I was *happier / happiest* when I passed my driving test than when I passed my exams.

7 The first day in my job was *more / most* worrying than my first day college.

Watch Out!

Learn the different forms of adjectives:

good ➜ *better* (comparative form) ➜ *best* (superlative form)

---

11 Read the statements below. Do you agree? Change the statements to make them true for you.

1 Studying in your hometown is better than studying in another town or country.

2 People who are getting married are happier than people who are coming of age.

3 Travelling on your own is more boring than travelling with others.

4 Passing a driving test is more exciting than passing exams at school.

5 The most important event for a student is end-of-year exams.

12 Complete the paragraph with the words below. There is one extra word.

> boring   felt   happier   most   nervous   than   the   wasn't   younger

For me, I think (1) .... most important event in my life was passing my driving test. I am (2) .... than all my friends and they all passed their test before me. I remember I was really (3) .... before each of my driving lessons. I (4) .... very good at the theory because I found it (5) .... I was (6) .... driving a car (7) .... reading about the rules. But when the day of the test came, I (8) .... confident.

Part 2: Skills development

Exam information

The Speaking test assesses your ability to use a range of relevant grammar to talk about the different IELTS topics.

Part 1

Exam tip

Listen carefully to the examiner's question in Part 1. What is the grammatical tense? Answer with the best tense: past, present or future.

1 Read the Part 1 questions and choose the correct answer (a or b). What is the mistake in the other answer?

1 Did you play any sports when you were a child?
   a Yes, I play lots of sports.
   b Yes, I played lots of sports.

2 What do you usually do on the internet?
   a I use the internet for chatting online and buying things.
   b I'm using the internet for chatting online and buying things.

3 Do you like travelling?
   a Yes, I love travelling. I'm going to go on a round-the-world trip next year and I'm really excited.
   b Yes, I love travelling. I'm going go on a round-the-world trip next year and I'm really excited.

4 Are you a student or do you have a job?
   a I'm a student. I've been a student at university since two years.
   b I'm a student. I've been a student at university for two years.

🔊 2 Listen to five Part 1 questions and choose the best beginning (a or b) for each answer.
67

1	a It was in …	b	It is in …
2	a I was …	b	I am …
3	a I watched …	b	I watch …
4	a I studied …	b	I'm studying …
5	a I chose …	b	I choose …

3 Now listen again and answer the questions.

4 Listen to your answers. Did you use the best tense? Use your answers in Exercise 2 to help you.

Part 2

5 Read the Part 2 task card below. Which grammatical phrases and tenses below would be relevant in your answer?

> present simple   past simple   *there is/are*   *there was/were*   *can/can't*
> present continuous   *have to*   *be going to*   should   present perfect

> **Describe an enjoyable event you experienced when you were at school.**
>
> You should say:
>
> **when it happened**
> **what was good about it**
> **who was there**
>
> And what made it enjoyable.

6 Listen to a model answer and read the audio script on page 97. How many grammatical phrases and tenses are in the answer?

68

7 Plan your answer in one minute. Then record your answer. Try to talk for one to two minutes.

Part 3

8 Read the Part 3 question and answer below. Match the underlined phrases with the grammatical tenses and phrases below.

1 obligation	**3** comparing	**5** future
2 present simple	**4** present continuous	

In your opinion, what are the most important events at school?

That's an interesting question. I think there are lots of important events. For example, the first day is an important event because you <u>meet</u> new friends and your teacher. You <u>have to</u> remember lots of names and new things. Tests are important too. Tests are usually <u>more difficult</u> at a new school. Finally, your last day at school <u>is</u> important. Thankfully, there are no more tests and you<u>'re going to</u> start a new job or go to university. In my opinion, you<u>'re starting</u> a new life. It's an important day to celebrate.

9 Read the Part 3 question in Exercise 8 again and record your answer. Which grammatical tenses and phrases did you use?

Exam tip

Listen to the grammatical tense in the Part 3 question and use this tense in the first part of your answer. Then use a range of grammatical phrases and tenses.

Part 3: Exam practice

Part 1

🔊 **1** **Listen to five Part 1 questions. Record your answer to each question.**
69

   1 Do you come from a large family?
   2 Did you have a favourite teacher at school?
   3 Do you have any hobbies?
   4 Describe your hometown.
   5 What's your experience of travelling to other countries?

Part 2

🔊 **2** **Listen to and read the Part 2 task card below. Plan your answer. You have one minute for**
70 **this in the exam. Then record your answer. You have one to two minutes for this in the exam.**

> **Describe an important event in your life.**
>
> You should say:
>
> **what the event was**
> **where and when it took place**
> **who was there**
>
> And explain what made it important to you.

3 **Answer the questions below to complete Part 2. Record your answer.**

   1 Do you think it's important to remember these types of event?
   2 Do you think planned events are more enjoyable than events that aren't planned?

Part 3

🔊 **4** **Listen to four Part 3 questions. Answer the questions and record your answers.**
71

Progress check

5 **Listen to your answers. Tick the boxes below to assess your answers.**

Do you ...
use a range of grammatical phrases and tenses in your answers? ☐
use vocabulary for talking about important events? ☐
use the correct endings of irregular verbs? ☐
use vocabulary for describing feelings? ☐
use intonation for giving emphasis? ☐
use comparing language? ☐

12 Possessions

AIMS: Describing objects • Pronunciation: linking words • Present perfect with *for* and *since* • Skills development: Using a range of grammar • Exam practice: Part 1, Part 2, and Part 3

Part 1: Language development

Vocabulary: objects

A   B C   D

1 Look at the photos above. Which of the objects do you own? Which would you like to own? Why?

2 Match some of the words below to the objects in the photos.

black	glass	green	large	leather	metal	modern
new	old-fashioned	plastic	red	silver	small	wood

3 Add the words from Exercise 2 to the table below.

size	age	colour	material

🔊 **4**
72
 Listen to two people talking about their favourite possessions. What is the object? Which words do they use to describe the objects?

Watch Out!

Put adjectives in the correct order:

(1) size, (2) age, (3) colour, (4) material: a small, brown, leather bag.

5 Choose an object from the photos or an object you own and make notes on the points below:

- size
- age
- colour
- material
- why you like it

Vocabulary: Describing objects

6 Match the sentence beginnings 1–6 with the groups of endings a–f.

1	I wear it	**a**	cotton / glass / metal
2	I got it for	**b**	carrying all my things / downloading music / studying and reading
3	It's made of	**c**	my birthday / my graduation / my wedding
4	It's important to me because	**d**	a brilliant holiday / a special day / my country
5	I use it for	**e**	every day / for special occasions / when I go on long trips
6	It reminds me of	**f**	I bought it on my first trip overseas / I saved up to buy it / my best friend gave it to me

7 Complete the descriptions below with the beginning of a sentence (1–6) in Exercise 6.

1 One of my favourite possessions is my laptop. .... chatting online or watching films with my friends.

2 I wear this necklace every day. .... my wedding day, because my husband bought it for me. It's very special.

3 I have a very large suitcase. I've had it since I was eighteen. .... I bought it for my first trip to America.

4 My mobile is important to me, It's small and .... metal and plastic. It's got lots of things on it – music, apps, photos and internet.

8 Look back at your notes from Exercise 5. Use the notes and the phrases from Exercise 6 to write a description.

Pronunciation: Linking words

9 Read and listen to the sentences below. Pay attention to the link ‿ between the two words.

1 It's made of leather.

2 I use it for texting my friends.

3 I like it because …

4 It's important to me because …

5 It reminds me of …

10 Listen again and repeat each sentence. Complete each sentence with your own ideas.

Exam tip

Practise linking consonant sounds and vowel sounds in your sentences to help you speak at a natural pace.

Grammar: Present perfect with *for* and *since*

🔊 **11** Listen and complete the sentences with the correct past participles and *for* or *since*.
74

    1 I've .... my mobile .... about three months.

    2 I've .... this guitar .... 2002.

    3 I've .... this laptop .... a year.

    4 I've .... this photo in my bag .... my graduation.

    5 I've .... this watch .... years.

    6 I've .... a new car .... I passed my driving test.

12 Answer the questions below. Use the present perfect with *for* or *since* in your answers.

What important object have you ...
... owned since you were a child?
... used for years?
... had for a few months?
... wanted since you were a teenager?

Watch Out!

Use the past simple for a finished event in the past.

I bought it last year.

---

13 Complete the text with the words below. There are two extra words.

bought	carry	favourite	had	important	it
green	modern	possessions	reminds	wear	

I've got lots of really great (1) .... But I think my (2) .... possession is my coat. I got (3) .... for my graduation and celebrate getting my degree. I've (4) .... it for two years. My parents (5) .... it for me and I was really surprised. It's beautiful. It's a (6) .... , black, leather coat. It's (7) .... to me because I know my parents were very proud. It (8) .... me of studying for my degree and my time at university. I only (9) .... it for special occasions because it's really expensive.

Part 2: Skills development

Exam information

In each part of the test you are assessed on four main points: (1) fluency and coherence (speaking without pauses and in an organized way), (2) accuracy and range of grammar, (3) accuracy and range of vocabulary and (4) pronunciation.

1 Complete the tips below on how to give answers with fluency and coherence.

> natural   notes   organize   pause

    1 Try not to .... when you are answering – speak at a ,............... pace.

    2 Make .... on each point on the task card.

    3 Include useful phrases to .... your answer.

2 Read the Part 2 task card below and plan your answer for one minute. Use the tips from Exercise 1 to help you. Then record your answer.

> ### Describe a gift you bought for someone.
>
> You should say:
>
> **what it was**
> **who you bought it for**
> **why you bought it**
>
> And say how you felt when you gave the gift.

3 Complete the tips below about how to demonstrate your range of grammar.

> carefully   choose   tenses

    1 Revise different grammatical .... and phrases from earlier units.

    2 Listen .... to the examiner's questions and .... suitable tenses for your answer.

4 Read the Part 3 questions below and think about your answers. Use the tips from Exercise 3 to help you. Then record your answers.

    1 Do you think going shopping with friends is a good way to relax?

    2 In your opinion, are there more advantages than disadvantages to studying in another country?

    3 How has looking for a job changed compared with in the past?

    4 How should we encourage people to be active in their free time?

5 Complete the tips below about how to demonstrate your range of vocabulary.

> adverbs   describing   repeat   similar   topic

    1 Revise .... vocabulary from earlier units.
    2 Do not .... words when you are .... something.
    3 Try to use words with .... meanings, e.g. adjectives or ....

6 Read the Part 2 task card below and plan your answer for one minute. Use the tips from Exercise 5 to help you. Then record your answer.

> **Talk about a photograph you took.**
>
> You should say:
>
> **when you took it**
> **who was there**
> **what it shows**
>
> And why you like this particular photograph.

7 Complete the tips below about how to demonstrate good pronunciation.

> clearly   model   pronunciation   repeat   stress   suitable

    1 Listen to the .... answers in the book and .... the answers. Try to sound like the speakers.
    2 Learn the correct .... and word .... of all new words.
    3 Practise using .... intonation in your answers.
    4 Remember to speak .... and at a natural pace.

8 Read the Part 1 and part 3 questions below and think about your answers. Use the tips from Exercise 10 to help you. Then record your answers.

    1 Can you describe your family?
    2 What do you like doing in your free time?
    3 Have you planned any holidays?
    4 Do you think your country is good for tourists?
    5 Many people think that young people today are not healthy. Do you agree?

Part 3: Exam practice

Part 1

🔊 **1**   Listen to five Part 1 questions. Record your answer to each question.
75

Part 2

🔊 **2**   Listen to and read the Part 2 task card below. Plan your answer. You have one minute for
76   this in the exam. Then record your answer. You have one to two minutes for this in the exam.

> **Describe something you own which is very important to you.**
>
> You should say:
>
> **what it is and what it looks like**
> **what it is made of**
> **how long you have had it**
>
> And explain why it is important to you.

3   Answer the questions below to complete Part 2. Record your answer.

     1   Would it be easy to replace this object?
     2   Do your friends like this object?

Part 3

🔊 **4**   Listen to four Part 3 questions. Answer the questions and record your answer.
77

Progress check

5   Listen to your answers. Tick the boxes below to assess your answers.

Do you ...
demonstrate fluency and coherence in your answers? ☐
include a range of vocabulary and grammar in your answers? ☐
use correct pronunciation and stress? ☐
speak clearly and use suitable intonation? ☐
use vocabulary for describing objects? ☐
use the present perfect with *for* and *since*? ☐

Review 4

1 Unscramble the words to make healthy activities.

1 do strops ....
2 do *oyag* ....
3 eat *lewl* ....
4 have a *aheltyh* diet ....

5 play a *sculiam* instrument ....
6 play board *sagem* ....
7 play *nirba* training games ....
8 sleep for eight *ushor* every night ....

2 Cross out the incorrect word in each sentence.

1 I like doing yoga. It's *hard / healthy / keep your mind active*.
2 It's important to *challenging / relax after college / work in a team*.
3 It makes me feel *great / happy / keep fit*.

3 Match topics (a–c) with two pieces of advice: one with *should* and one with *shouldn't*.

a getting fit

b healthy diet

c feeling stressed

1 Doing yoga makes me feel relaxed. You should try it.
2 You should always eat well.
3 You shouldn't drive everywhere. You can walk or cycle.
4 You shouldn't study late at night. It's bad for you.
5 You shouldn't eat junk food. It's bad for you.
6 You should try to do more exercise.

4 Complete the important events with the missing word.

1 c .... of age
2 g .... married
3 g .... your first job
4 g .... from university
5 t .... on your own for the first time
6 w .... a sports competition

5 Add the words to the table.

bored   delighted   excited   happy   nervous   relaxed   satisfied   terrified   tired

positive feelings	
negative feelings	

6 **Complete the comparing sentences with a word from the box.**

are	is	more	than	the

  1 Students in their final year .... happier than students in their first year.
  2 Winning a sports competition is better .... passing an exam.
  3 Applying for college courses is .... boring than applying for jobs.
  4 Getting your first job .... more exciting than starting college.
  5 One of .... most important events for a student is the graduation ceremony.

7 **Put the adjectives in the correct order to describe the objects.**

  1 A .... coat. (brown, large, leather)
  2 A .... mobile phone. (modern, plastic, small)
  3 A .... watch. (metal, new, red)
  4 A .... necklace. (green, old-fashioned, small)

8 **Complete the sentences with the words in the box.**

for	got	important	made	me	use

  1 It's .... of wood and glass.
  2 I wear it .... special occasions.
  3 I .... it for my birthday.
  4 It's .... to me because I bought it on holiday.
  5 I .... it for chatting online.
  6 It reminds .... of my family and my country.

9 **Correct the mistakes in the present perfect sentences. There is one correct sentence.**

  1 I've own it for five years.
  2 I wanted a phone since I was ten years old.
  3 I've wore it every day since I got it.
  4 I've use my computer for two years.
  5 I've had it since three years.
  6 I carry it in my bag since my graduation.
  7 I've be to England three times.
  8 I've had this coat since my birthday.

Practice test

Listen to the examiner and answer the questions in each part.

 Part 1

78

1 Do you work or are you a student?
2 Do you have a large family?
3 Describe your hometown.
4 What's the weather like in your country?
5 What are some of your hobbies?

 Part 2

79

> **Describe a person who helped you.**
>
> You should say:
>
> **where you met the person**
> **what relationship this person was to you**
> **what was special about them**
>
> And explain how this person helped you.
> Would you like to help someone in this way?

 Part 3

80

1 Do you think we can learn anything from older generations?
2 Compare the role of the family in today's world to the past.
3 Should we ask our family for help, or should we try being independent?
4 In your opinion, when does a child become an adult?

Audio scripts

Unit 1   Family

Track 01

brother
father
grandfather

Track 02

brother
mother
grandmother

Track 03

1   My mother is very kind. She loves everybody!
    She looks like her sister. They've both got curly
    hair. My mum is a creative person. She makes
    things all the time.

2   I don't have any brothers or sisters. I'm
    an only child. But I've got seven aunts! My
    favourite aunt is called Betty. She's very clever.
    She's a teacher and she helps me with my
    studies.

3   My uncle is so bossy. He tells me what to
    do all the time! He is married and his wife is
    bossy too. But their son is really funny! He's my
    favourite cousin. We go to the same college.

Track 04

My family? Well, we're a big family actually. Our
house is large! I've got five brothers. Their names
are Carlos, Gino, Luca, Alex and Marco. Carlos is
14 and he's the youngest. He's good looking and
very funny. Marco is 27 and he's the oldest. His wife
teaches at my college. Her name is Maria.
    My mother is an only child, so her family is very
small. But my father is from a big family. He has
three brothers. He looks like his brother, my uncle
Georgio. They are both bossy but kind. My uncle has
four children and one cat. Its name is Lola.
    Tell me about your family.

Track 05

Hello. My name is Steve Smith. Could you tell me
    your full name, please?
Thank you. Can you show me your identification,
    please?

I'd now like to ask you some questions about
    yourself. Tell me about your family.
What does your father do?
How much time do you spend with your family?
Are people in your country close to their family?
Do you prefer to go out with your family or your
    friends?
Where do you live at the moment?

Track 06

My father is a doctor. He helps people. He works in
a hospital. He's very kind to people.

Track 07

What do you do?
How would you describe your family?
Who is important to you in your family?

Unit 2   Free time

Track 08

1   I love using the Internet. My brother is at
    university in England, so I really like chatting
    online with him. He's very funny. I enjoy playing
    computer games with my friends. My computer
    is very important to me.

2   I study long hours every day, so I don't have
    much free time. I prefer doing nothing to
    doing exercise. I don't like going to the gym.
    It's boring. I enjoy relaxing and reading
    magazines.

3   It depends. Sometimes I like doing exercise.
    Sometimes I like going for walks. My favourite
    thing is going shopping at the weekends. It's
    relaxing and good fun.

Track 09

1   I love using the Internet.

2   I really like chatting online with him.

3   I prefer doing nothing to doing exercise.

4   I don't like going to the gym.

5   It depends. Sometimes I like going for walks.

6   My favourite thing is going shopping.

Track 10

Now I'm going to give you a topic and I'd like you to talk about it for one to two minutes. You'll have one minute to think about what you're going to say before you begin talking. You can make some notes if you wish. Here is a pencil and some paper. I'd like you to describe a newspaper or magazine you enjoy reading. You should say what kind of newspaper or magazine it is, which parts of it you read, when and where you read it, and explain why you enjoy reading it.

Track 11

I enjoy reading a magazine called *Fab Football*. It is about sport, of course, and it's my favourite sport. I love watching football from different countries and I love reading about it.

The magazine's got lots of good information. I don't like reading the letters or adverts. I prefer reading the interviews with famous players, or the news.

I read *Fab Football* every weekend. I buy it on Saturday morning and go home and read.

I enjoy meeting friends and reading the magazine together. I don't mind sharing it. We like chatting about the news, the players. It's very interesting.

Track 12

Now I'm going to give you a topic and I'd like you to talk about it for one to two minutes. You'll have one minute to think about what you're going to say before you begin talking. You can make some notes if you wish. Here is a pencil and some paper. I'd like you to describe an activity that you like doing. You should say what activity it is, when and where you do it, who you like doing it with, and explain why you enjoy doing it.

Unit 3   Special occasions

Track 13

Last year I travelled to Rio and visited my cousin and his family. My best friend went too.

We went to my cousin's house and we had a delicious traditional meal. After we ate dinner, we walked to the city centre. When we saw the carnival, it was very exciting! We danced and sang. We watched the parade. It was fun, but we were very tired. Then we visited another city and stayed at a famous hotel, but it wasn't very nice. We stayed for two days then we went home. It was a special trip for me because I travelled without my parents for the first time.

Track 14

/t/
danced
watched

/d/
stayed
travelled

/ɪd/
hated
visited

Track 15

1   liked

2   loved

3   started

4   studied

5   walked

6   wanted

Track 16

1   Is it important for a country to have festivals?

2   Are friends more important than family?

Track 17

What is an important festival in your country?
What are your favourite parts of this festival?
How have special occasions such as weddings
   changed in your country?
Do you think special occasions and festivals are
   important for a society?

Review 1

Track 18

1   I don't like reading magazines.

2   I really like going to the gym.

3   My favourite thing is chatting online.

Unit 4   Hometown

Track 19

one syllable: beach, bridge, park
two syllables: café, hotel, river
three syllables: factory, gallery, skyscraper, theatre

Track 20

café
hotel
river
factory
gallery
skyscraper
theatre

Track 21

There is a museum, yes. It's very famous. Culture is important to my city. So there are lots of tourist attractions such as galleries, tours, theatres, that sort of thing. There's lots of traffic in the centre. Everybody has a car! There are some shopping malls, which is good because I love going shopping with my friends. There are always lots of people in the malls. And there are some traditional food markets. You can buy lots of strange food there. There isn't a beach but it doesn't matter. And there aren't any harbours. One problem is that there isn't any accommodation for students. It's very difficult to study here.

Track 22

Yes, I like the capital city. I like this very much.

I live in the capital city. I know it very well. It is in the north of my country. It is very nice. It's got lots of business and lots of tourists. There's a beach in the city and you can see mountains. People shop in the city and people work in the city.

I like it because it's my hometown. It is clean. It is modern. I like living there.

Track 23

a   I'm a student. I'm studying Business.

b   In my country, I see my family everyday. We all live together. In London, it isn't possible. I see my uncle sometimes.

c   There are many jobs. People can work in factories, schools, or offices. There are lots of international businesses, too.

d   The subject is very interesting. I want a good job in my country and I can get a promotion with this qualification. The exams are difficult but I'm improving.

e   It's OK. It's the same as other countries, I think.

f   Beijing is in the north of China.

g   No, there is a problem with traffic. The roads are always busy and pollution is bad.

Unit 5   TV and radio

Track 24

1   I enjoy listening to a programme called *Fashion Today*. It's a documentary series. It's about clothes and the fashion industry. It's presented by different models each week. I like learning about the different fashions.

2   In my country, reality TV shows are very popular. My favourite show is *Hello Hotel*. The participants are famous people. They work in the hotel. The thing I like best is the hotel manager. He's always angry.

3   I often watch a drama series called *Patrol*. It's set in London. It stars some famous actors. It's about the police. It's very exciting. I think it's good entertainment.

Unit 6   Weather

Track 25

uː
monsoon
aʊ
now
ʌ
summer
eɪ
favourite
ɔː
stormy
əʊ
cold

Track 26

April
autumn

drought
humid
June
month
November
outside
rainy
snowy
stormy
sunny

Track 27

uː
humid
June

ɑʊ
drought
outside

ʌ
month
sunny

eɪ
April
rainy

ɔː
autumn
stormy

əʊ
November
snowy

Track 28

1   You can go to the beach in the summer.

2   You can't do anything when the weather is very hot.

3   You can't play tennis outside when it's rainy.

4   The rainy season can last for weeks.

5   You can't go skiing in hot and dry climates.

6   The weather can change quickly in the mountains.

Track 29

1
How many seasons does your country have?
My country has four seasons.

2
What's your favourite season of the year?
Summer. This is my favourite season.

3
How do rainy days make you feel?
I feel very sad on rainy days.

4
What do you like doing when it's hot?
I like going to the beach.

Unit 7   Studying

Track 30

1   I'm studying medicine. It's hard work and there are lots of lectures, but I enjoy helping people. I'm in my first year and I'd like to be a doctor.

2   I'm doing a business studies course. I'm learning about all the different parts of a business. This semester I'm learning about finance and marketing. It's really interesting. I'd like to be a company director.

3   I'm studying law, so I'm learning about the legal system. It's a very difficult course and there are lots of deadlines. I'd like to be a lawyer.

Track 31

1   business, two syllables, business

2   literature, three syllables, literature

3   mathematics, four syllables, mathematics

4   university, five syllable, university

Track 32

chemistry
college
deadline
engineering
graduate
graduation
history
lecture
medicine
presentation
project
timetable

Track 33

1 [O o]
business
college

deadline
lecture
project

2 [O o o]
chemistry
literature
graduate
history
medicine
timetable

3 [o o O o]
mathematics
engineering
graduation
presentation

4 [o o O o o]
university

Track 34

1 Marcel
I'm revising for an exam. It's my final year and I'm working very hard. I'm having extra tuition, and my grades are improving.

2 Dee
I'm visiting my brother at college. He's living in halls this year, and he's having a great time. I'm helping him with his coursework this semester, and we're preparing a presentation at the moment.

3 Lara
I'm thinking about doing another course next year. I'm applying for a scholarship at a university in my hometown, and I'm filling out the application form now.

Track 35

Yes, yes they are. My father and my brother studied law at university and they think it is a very nice subject. My mother thinks it is nice and always asks me questions about law. I have lots of friends on the course and we want to get a nice job when we graduate.

Track 36

Yes, yes they are. My father and my brother studied law at university and they think it is a very important subject. My mother thinks it is interesting and always asks me questions about law. I have lots of friends on the course and we want to get a good job when we graduate.

Track 37

1 No, I don't think so. Unfortunately, I think lots of changes were made to the education system last year and teachers and professors aren't happy. They want more money for the schools and universities, but the government can't give them more money.

2 Yes, definitely. I live with my family. I enjoy living at home because I can relax and just study. For example, my parents cook meals, wash my clothes and clean my room. I can spend more time studying and I think this is good.

3 My parents went to a school in my hometown. The school is a very popular one and they enjoyed it. I went to school in anther country and I didn't like living away from home. My father went to university but I don't think there were lots of universities in my country at the time. Fortunately, there are lots of universities and colleges there today. I'm visiting different universities at the moment because I'm choosing which course to study next year.

Track 38

1 What are you studying now?

2 Why did you choose that subject?

3 Do you enjoy it? Why?

4 What is the best thing about studying?

5 Are there many jobs for you after you finish studying?

Track 39

1 Do you think young children enjoy going to school and learning?

2 Is it a good idea to live with your family when you are studying?

3 Compare your experience of education to your parents' generation.

4 Many people think there are benefits to studying in another country. Do you agree?

5 Do you think your country has a good education system?

Unit 8 Work

Track 40

1 I'm a police officer and I work different shifts each week. My job is to keep people safe.

2 I work for a national newspaper. I interview people and write articles. I'm a journalist.

3 I help my patients every day. I work in a hospital and I'm a nurse.

4 I work as a volunteer. I work with animals and I have to look after them every day.

5 I'm a businessman and I work in the city. I work with different companies and I make lots of money.

6 I work in a school and my job is to help students pass exams. I'm a teacher.

Track 41

a I had a part-time job at the company and I really enjoyed it. My boss and my colleagues were professional but very friendly. I applied for a full-time job in my final year at university and I got it. The job is well-paid, so I'm earning a good salary, and I also travel to lots of different countries. It's an exciting job.

b I work as a personal assistant at a very well-known company. I love my job. I got my job last year. I worked here as a volunteer to get work experience. I really enjoyed it so I wrote to the company director and asked for a job. I use my languages regularly, and I work flexible hours.

c Two years ago, I worked as a volunteer in a hospital because I wanted to help people. I went to university, but I worked at the hospital each summer. I didn't want to travel the world, so I applied for the job. Now I'm earning a good salary, and it's my dream job!

Track 42

What do you do?
I'm a manager. I work for a well-known international company, so I often have to travel to different offices around the world.

Did you have to get any qualifications or do any training for your job?

Yes, I did. I had to complete three training courses. Thankfully, I didn't have to revise for any exams because the assessment was an interview and giving a presentation.

Do you have to wear a uniform or smart clothes?
I don't have to wear a uniform, but I have to wear a suit to meetings.

Do you have to work long hours?
Yes. At the moment, I need to work hard to complete a project.

What does your job involve?
Well, I have to meet lots of people, but I don't have to speak different languages because we all speak English. I often have to prepare reports or give presentations.

Track 43

That's an interesting question. Let me think. I definitely think that work experience is an important way to learn about a job. I studied business for three years and I graduated with honours. Then I got a good job, but it was really hard work and tiring. I suppose that your first job is always difficult. I learnt lots in my first year there. But my course did help me, for example I understood lots of basic points about business and finance. There are pros and cons. Work experience is an excellent way to learn about a job in real life, but education or training gives you time to learn the theories.

Track 44

That's interesting. Let me see. I think my parents didn't have lots of choices. They worked in their hometown or maybe the capital city. I guess that they wrote letters to apply for jobs advertised in the local newspaper. I don't think my parents' generation usually travelled for work. I'm not sure. But I can apply for jobs anywhere in the world. I look for jobs online and email application forms from my laptop. So I think it's easy for my generation. There are advantages and disadvantages, because today I have lots of different opportunities and it's sometimes difficult to make a decision.

Track 45

1 In your opinion, do people work more now than in the past?

2 Do you think companies need people to travel to an office and work there, or can people work from home?

Unit 9   Holidays and travel

Track 46

I'm going to go on an activity holiday next month. I'm very excited. I'm going to America. I like Americans. I think the people are very friendly.

I'm going to learn new sports, like basketball and American football. I think both sports are very exciting. I'm also going to take lessons in water sports, but I'm not going to go swimming in the sea because I'm not a very good swimmer.

I'm not going to go sightseeing, but I'm going to visit local festivals and I'm going to eat in traditional restaurants. The food is going to be delicious.

I'm going to go on day trips because there are some beautiful places in America.

Track 47

1   I'm going **to** study in America.

2   I'm going **to** study in America.

Track 48

1   I'm going to visit England.

2   I'm not going to visit Spain.

Track 49

1   I'm going to stay in a hotel.

2   I'm not going to take any photos.

3   I'm going to eat in traditional restaurants.

4   We're going to visit historical sites.

5   We're not going to learn a new sport.

6   We're going to go sightseeing.

Track 50

Do you have lots of close friends?

Track 51

1   Do you think holidays and travelling were more important in the past?

2   In your opinion, is it a good idea for families to work together?

3   Many people think there are benefits to studying in another country. Do you agree?

4   Compare your experience of finding a job to your parents' generation.

Track 52

1   When was your last holiday?

2   Do you like travelling? Why? Why not?

3   What kinds of places do you like visiting?

4   Is there a country you would like to visit?

5   Do you think tourists enjoy visiting your country?

Track 53

1   Compare your experience of holidays and travelling with your parents' generation.

2   Many people think it is a good idea to go on holiday in your own country. Do you agree?

3   In your opinion, is it important to speak the language of the country you're visiting?

4   Do you think travelling with friends is a good way to travel?

Review 3

Track 54

1   I'm going to learn new sports. I'd like to go skiing.

2   I'm not going to go swimming in the sea because I can't swim.

3   I'm going to go sightseeing. There are lots of tourist attractions.

4   I'm not going to visit local festivals. I think they've boring.

5   I'm going to eat in traditional restaurants. I enjoy trying new food.

6   I'm going to take lots of photos because I've got a new camera.

Unit 10   Health

Track 55

I like doing yoga and playing brain training games. I enjoy doing these activities on my own, because I work in a busy, noisy office every day. It's important to relax after a hard day. Yoga makes me feel relaxed and I think brain training games are good for my mind.

Track 56

Charles
I like playing chess. I spend lots of time playing chess with my father. I think it's good for you. It's good for your mind because it's challenging and you have to think and plan all the time. It's hard! In my opinion, it's important to keep your mind active.

Rosa
A healthy activity I enjoy doing is cooking. I cook every day because I think it's important to have a healthy diet. You shouldn't' eat junk food because it's not good for you. I like cooking at home and inviting friends and family for dinner. It makes me feel happy because everybody thinks the food is delicious.

Track 57

1   It's good for you.

2   It isn't good for you.

3   It's really bad for you.

4   It's important to stay healthy.

5   You shouldn't eat junk food.

Track 58

1   Compare the differences between sports now and in the past.

2   In your opinion, do you think relaxing is an important part of being healthy?

3   How can we encourage young people to be healthy?

Track 59

1   Compare the differences between sports now and in the past.
    That's interesting. I think it's important to play sports. There are lots of different sports now and you can learn a new sport wherever you live. Sports people earn a good salary. I think it's a good job. I'd like to be a professional golfer. But there are some boring sports. For example, I don't like watching motor racing.

2   In your opinion, do you think relaxing is an important part of being healthy?
    Definitely. I think relaxing is a very important part of being healthy. We are always busy. We're travelling to work or college, we're meeting friends, we're doing homework. So in my opinion, I think it's important to slow down and relax. It is good for our bodies and our minds.

3   How can we encourage young people to be healthy?
    That's a difficult question. Let me see. Unfortunately, in my country, young people like playing computer games and they usually like eating junk food. We should encourage them to play game outdoors. For example, they could go to the beach and do water sports. We should encourage them to learn about food and cook some healthy food with their families.

Track 60

1   In your opinion, what are the main advantages of children's games?

2   How can a school help students have healthy lives?

3   Do you think there is more opportunity to learn sports now than in the past?

Track 61

1   What do you like doing in your free time?

2   Do you enjoy watching sports?

3   Do you enjoy participating in any sports?

4   Which sports are most popular in your country?

5   How much time do you spend on your hobbies?

Track 62

1   Compare the differences between sports now and in the past.

2   In your opinion, do people in your country eat better or worse nowadays?

3   How can we encourage young people to be healthy?

4   Do you think a country's government should help people to be healthy?

Unit 11   Important events

Track 63

I remember getting to the airport and feeling really nervous. I had lots of bags, my passport, my currency and I looked for the check-in desk. Then I couldn't find my ticket but my mother had it in her bag. My parents came with me to say goodbye. They knew it was an important day for me because I was travelling on my own for the first time. I checked in my luggage and then I felt very excited.

Track 64

I was very nervous before the national championships. I felt terrified! We travelled to the city the night before and it was a long and boring journey on the bus. We were all really tired when we woke up the next day. Finally, our match started. I was surprised because some of the players on my team were very relaxed. The opposition were an excellent team and the match was tiring, but thankfully we won! We were all delighted and I think our manager was satisfied with the result. It was a really exciting event for me.

Track 65

1   I was very bored at my brother's graduation

2   I feel really tired at the end of the week.

3   I was very surprised when I passed all my exams.

4   I felt really excited when I travelled on my own.

Track 66

I think the most important event for a student is graduation day. It is more important than end-of-year exams because you are celebrating the end of university. I think graduates are happier than undergraduates because there are no more exams. Finding a job is more worrying than taking exams.

Track 67

1   When was your last holiday?

2   What do you do?

3   What do you usually watch on TV?

4   What are you studying now?

5   Why did you choose that subject?

Track 68

I'd like to talk about an enjoyable event I experienced when I was at school.

It happened in my senior school and I was about fifteen or sixteen years old. There was a story writing competition in the local newspaper and my teacher said I should enter it. I really enjoyed writing stories and poems, so I wrote a story and I entered the competition. I was very nervous, but thankfully I won! I was really surprised.

It was good because I won some money and some books. It made me more confident about studying, too. I applied for college after winning the competition.

I went to the presentation ceremony in my hometown. I went with my parents and my sister. There were lots of people there, and there was a photographer taking photos. It was one of the most exciting days of my life.

Finally, it was enjoyable because my parents were very proud and we celebrated with a party at home. I often look at the photo from the competition. I've had the photo on my bookcase for about six years. It's very special to me.

Track 69

1   Do you come from a large family?

2   Did you have a favourite teacher at school?

3   Do you have any hobbies?

4   Describe your hometown.

5   What's your experience of travelling to other countries?

Track 70

I'd like you to describe an important event in your life. You should say what the event was, where and when it took place, who was there at the time and explain what made it important to you.

Track 71

1   Compare how important events, like weddings, have changed compared to your parents' generation.

2   In your opinion, how should people remember important events from their country's past?

3   How do schools in your country help pupils prepare for events like sports competitions or end-of-year exams?

4   Many people think photos are the best way to remember special occasions. Do you agree?

Unit 12   Possessions

Track 72

One of my favourite possessions is my electric guitar. It was very expensive and it was a birthday present for my eighteenth birthday. My grandparents gave it to me. It's modern and red and white. I play it every day. I think it's made of wood and plastic. I like it because my grandparents gave it to me and my birthday was a very special day.

One of my favourite possessions is a handbag. It's large, old-fashioned, and it's made of red leather. I love it. It's beautiful. My older sister gave it to me when I graduated. I like it because it reminds me of my graduation, and I use it for carrying all my things.

Track 73

1   It's made of leather.

2   I use it for texting my friends.

3   I like it because it's unusual.

4   It's important to me because my father gave it to me.

5   It reminds me of home.

Track 74

1   I've had my mobile for about three months.

2   I've owned this guitar since 2002.

3   I've used this laptop for a year.

4   I've carried this photo in my bag since my graduation.

5   I've worn this watch for years.

6   I've wanted a new car since I passed my driving test.

Track 75

1   Which country are you from?

2   Which is the most popular place to go shopping in your hometown?

3   How often do you shop online?

4   When did you last buy a present for someone?

5   What do you like doing when you go out?

Track 76

I'd like you to describe something you own which is very important to you. You should say what it is and what it looks like, what it is made of, how long you have had it and explain why it is important to you.

Track 77

1   In your opinion, do possessions make people happy?

2   Compare the important possessions you have with the important possessions your parents have.

3   Many people think that shopping is a good way to relax. Do you agree?

4   Is it better to receive a present or to give a present?

Practice test

Track 78

Good morning. My name is Katy Green. Can you tell me your full name please?
Thank you. Can I see your identification, please?
Thank you, that's fine
Now I'd like to ask you some questions about yourself.
Do you work or are you a student?
Do you have a large family?
Describe your hometown.
What's the weather like in your country?
What are some of your hobbies?

Track 79

Now, I'm going to give you a topic and I'd like you to talk about it for one to two minutes. Before you talk, you'll have one minute to think about what you're going to say. You can make some notes if you wish. Do you understand?

I'd like you to describe a person who helped you. You should say, where you met the person, what relationship this person was to you, what was special about them and explain how this person helped you.

Would you like to help someone in this way?

Track 80

We've been talking about a person who you admire, and now I'd like to ask you some more general questions about people.
Do you think we can learn anything from older generations?
Compare the role of the family in today's world to the past.
Should we ask our family for help, or should we try being independent?
In your opinion, when does a child become an adult?

Answer key

Unit 1   Family

Part 1:   Language development

Vocabulary: Family

Exercise 1

1 sister

2 brothers

3 parents

4 mother, wife

5 daughter, sons

6 grandparents, husband

Exercise 2

1 sister

2 brother

3 mother

4 father

Pronunciation: /ð/

Exercise 5

brother

mother

grandmother

Vocabulary: Describing people

Exercise 6

bossy, calm, clever, confident, creative, friendly, funny, happy, kind

Students' own answers.

Exercise 7

1 clever

2 bossy

3 confident

4 calm

5 friendly, funny

Exercise 8

Speaker 1: kind, creative

Speaker 2: clever

Speaker 3: bossy, funny

Exercise 9

Speaker 1: looks

Speaker 2: brothers

Speaker 3: favourite

Grammar: Possessive adjectives

Exercise 11

1 Our

2 Their

3 His

4 Her

5 her

6 my

7 Its

8 your

Exercise 12

I	you	he	she	it	we	they
my	your	his	her	its	our	their

Part 2:   Skills development

Exercise 1

1 d	4 e
2 b	5 c
3 a	

Exercise 2

1 name

2 full name

3 identification

4 family

5 do

6 How

7 country

8 friends

9 live

Exercise 3
What does your father do?

Exercise 4
1 Most is relevant, but some is not relevant: *He's very kind to people.*

2 OK.

3 at normal speed

4 relevant: *doctor, helps, people, hospital;* not relevant: *kind to people*

5 clear

6 no errors

Part 3:   Exam practice
Exercise 1

Model answer:
1 I'm from Dubai. It's in the United Arab Emirates.

2 No, it's a small family. I'm an only child. There are my parents and my grandmother.

3 My mother is a manager in an office.
4 Yes, we live in a big flat in the centre of the city.

Exercise 2
What do you do?
How would you describe your family?
Who is important to you in your family?

Model answer:
1 I'm a teacher. I work in a language school.

2 My family is large. I have two brothers and three sisters. My parents have got lots of brothers and sisters too.

3 My father is important to me. He works every day but he always helps me with my studies. We like going for walks together.

Unit 2   Free time

Part 1:   Language development

Vocabulary: Free time activities

Exercise 1
A chatting online

B reading magazines

C jogging

D going shopping

Exercise 2
doing: exercise, nothing
going: to the gym, for walks
playing: football, tennis
watching: a DVD, TV

Vocabulary: Expressing preferences

Exercise 5
Speaker 1: using the Internet, playing computer
   games
Speaker 2: doing nothing, reading magazines
Speaker 3: going shopping, going for walks

Exercise 6
1 I love

2 I really like

3 I prefer

4 I don't like

5 It depends

6 My favourite thing

Grammar: Present simple

Exercise 8
1 a   3 b   5 a

2 b   4 a

Part 2:   Skills development

Exercise 2
1 magazine

2 sport

3 interviews, news

4 the weekend

5 home

6 It's very interesting.

Exercise 3
1 newspaper or magazine

2 which parts

3 when

4 what kind

5 explain why

6 where

Part 3:   Exam practice

Exercise 1
Key words: activity, like, where, when, who with, why

Exercise 2

Model answer:
Activity: watching DVDs
Where: home or at brother's flat
When: every weekend
Who with: my family
Why: relaxing, spend time with my family, eating

Exercise 3

Model answer:
The activity I like doing is watching DVDs. I love
watching films. I watch DVDs every weekend and
sometimes in the week. I prefer watching films
at home to going to the cinema. I watch films at
my brother's flat too. I like watching films with my
family. We cook a meal and then we enjoy eating
and watching a funny film. It's fun and I like
spending time with my family.

Unit 3 Special occasions

Part 1: Language development
Vocabulary: Special occasions
Exercise 1
A family, balloons

B fireworks

C carnival, costumes, parade

Exercise 2
1 give

2 make

3 family

4 presents

5 parade

6 wear

7 watch

8 fireworks

Vocabulary: Connecting ideas
Exercise 3
1 d	4 e
2 f	5 b
3 c	6 a

Exercise 4
1 but

2 then

3 too

4 After

5 because

6 When

Grammar: Past simple
Exercise 5
1 ate

2 gave

3 made

4 met

5 wore

6 saw

Exercise 6
1 went

2 graduated

3 was

4 danced

5 didn't stay

6 were

Pronunciation: Past simple verbs and -ed
Exercise 8
/t/
liked
walked

/d/
loved
studied

/ɪd/
started
wanted

Exercise 9
1 met, watched, travelled, but

2 wore, played, when, saw

Part 2: Skills development
Exercise 1
a 3	c 1
b 2	

Exercise 2
a 3	c 1
b 2	

Exercise 3
1 Is it important for a country to have festivals?

2 Are friends more important than family?

Exercise 5

1 Is it important for a country to have festivals?

Exercise 6

1 a Yes

 b Yes

2 a Yes, the speaker also extends the answer to include *other countries.*

 b No, the speaker talks about a personal experience of a festival not about the importance of a country having festivals.

3 a Yes, I think, yes. <u>In my country</u>, we have one or two big festivals. We visit family or we remember people or events. It is <u>important</u>. It is a serious thing but it is fun. I like travelling to <u>other countries</u> for festivals too. It is interesting to learn about the world.

 b I went to a <u>festival</u> in my country last year and I enjoyed it. It was <u>important to me</u> because I saw my friends and family.

4 a seven sentences

 b two sentences

Part 3: Exam practice

Part 2

Exercise 1

Model answer:
Special occasion: graduation
where: university, England
when: last summer
who: my family
explain how you felt: excited, nervous

Exercise 2

Model answer:
My special occasion was my graduation ceremony. There was a parade with the professors and the other students. Then we went into a hall for the ceremony and we got our certificates.

I graduated in England from Oxford University. It was last summer. It was very hot. My family flew to England for the ceremony and we celebrated together. I was very excited because my family came to visit me. I was nervous too. It was a very important day.

Part 3

Exercise 4

Model answer:
What is an important festival in your country?
An important festival in my country is New Year. There is a big parade and a carnival. Tourists visit the city and watch the festival. It is a special evening.

What are your favourite parts of this festival?

My favourite parts of the festival are the music and the clothes. I enjoy watching the parade and the beautiful costumes. I really like singing and dancing to the music. It's fun.

How have special occasions such as weddings changed in your country?

I think that weddings are the same. I live in a traditional country and we have the same traditions today. The family go to a special building for the wedding ceremony. Then there are two or three other meals for other family and friends.

Do you think special occasions and festivals are important for a society?

Yes, it is important for people to learn about their country. I think it is interesting to learn about a different society too. When you go to a festival, you remember special events in the past and you celebrate. It is important to celebrate special occasions with your family and people from your country – it makes you happy.

Review 1

Exercise 1
1 husband

2 daughter

3 brother

4 grandmother

5 grandson

Exercise 2
1 kind

2 bossy

3 creative

4 confident

5 friendly

Exercise 3
1 My

2 your

3 Her

4 my

5 His

Exercise 4
1 the Internet

2 boring

3 magazines

4 to the gym

5 to music

Exercise 5
1 a   2 b   3 b

Exercise 6
1 I **really like** playing computer games.

2 Children in my country don't like **going** shopping.

3 My brother and I **like** going to museums.

4 I **don't** like going for walks.

Exercise 7
1 at

2 on

3 at

Exercise 8
give presents
visit family
watch fireworks
wear a costume

Exercise 9
1 but

2 Then

3 After

4 too

5 When

6 because

Exercise 10
1 visited, was

2 were, didn't like

3 sang, danced

4 graduated, got

5 didn't go, was

Unit 4 Hometown

Part 1: Language development

Vocabulary: Places in cities

Exercise 1

A harbour

B shopping mall

C museum

Exercise 2

Model answers:
harbour: go on a boat trip, have a coffee
shopping mall: buy clothes, have a coffee
museum: have a coffee, see an exhibition

Exercise 3

Model answers:
1 café, hotel (restaurant)

2 beach, river (harbour)

3 beach, café, gallery, theatre (cinema)

4 skyscraper (office)

5 bridge, skyscraper (hill)

Vocabulary: Describing cities

Exercise 4

1 c   4 d

2 a   5 b

3 c

Exercise 5

Model answers:
1 modern, beautiful

2 airport, mountains

3 lots of tourist attractions

4 traditional food, museums

5 the weather is good

Pronunciation: Syllables and word stress

Exercise 7

one syllable: beach, bridge, park
two syllables: cafe, hotel, river
three syllables: factory, gallery, skyscraper,
   theatre

Exercise 8

two syllables: cafe, hotel, river
three syllables: factory, gallery, skyscraper,
   theatre

Grammar: *There is / There are*

Exercise 9

There is (a) museum, (lots of) traffic
There isn't (a) beach, (any) accommodation
There are (some) shopping malls, (lots of) people,
   markets
There aren't (any) harbours

Exercise 10

1 are

2 isn't

3 are not

4 Are

5 No

6 are

7 aren't

Exercise 11

1 near

2 famous

3 got

4 skyscrapers

5 bridge

6 favourite

7 can

8 traditional

9 meet

10 are

Part 2: Skills development

Exercise 1

Good: The grammar is correct and the vocabulary
   is appropriate for the topic.
Bad: The answer is too short for Part 1.

Exercise 2

Possible answers:
- near the border, population 100,000

- clean, exciting, friendly

- museums, theatres

- very friendly, people always kind

Exercise 4

The answer is too fast. There are some pauses.
There are no grammar errors. Some words are
repeated, e.g. capital city, I like, people.

Exercise 7

- description of my country

- other cities I like
  The topic card does not ask for this information
  and it will waste time.

Part 3: Exam practice

Part 1

Exercise 1

1 a   5 c

2 d   6 g

3 b   7 e

4 f

Part 2

Exercise 4

Model answer:
Yes, last week I went to Dubai and I was there
because I was visiting my best friend. So what
I really like about Dubai was the fact that I was
there visiting my friend and I found it very, a very
great place. It's not so far from my country, first
of all, and it is in the UAE. It is near Abu Dhabi
and I flew to the airport there. My friend, he

met me, and we drove to Dubai. It was maybe
one hour until the outskirts, then the traffic was
very bad. In Dubai, you have to take the car
everywhere. We relaxed and went to the shopping
malls, they are great, and the beaches. We
chatted mainly. We haven't seen each other for
long time. And we went skiing! In the shopping
mall there is a slope. It was interesting because
it has many contrasts, because you have lots of
poor people and lots of very, very rich people.
There is no middle class there and the places
you go, there is gold, too much gold and, on the
other hand there are many people living there,
they are immigrants.

Unit 5   TV and radio

Part 1:   Language development
Vocabulary: Types of programme
Exercise 1
1 B

2 extra description

3 C

4 A

5 extra description

6 D

Vocabulary: Describing programmes
Exercise 3
a Speaker 1

b Speaker 3

c Speaker 2

Exercise 4

a 1		e 2	
b 3		f 3	
c 1		g 3	
d 3		h 2	

It's very exciting.
I think it's good entertainment.
The thing I like best is the hotel manager.

Grammar: Adverbs of frequency
Exercise 6

1 e	4 d
2 f	5 a
3 c	6 b

Exercise 7
1 rarely

2 often

3 always

Exercise 9
1 favourite, every, contestants, by

2 about, interesting, operas, actors

3 series, always, stars, exciting

4 talk, funny, contestants, sometimes

Part 2:   Skills development
Part 2
Exercise 1
type of programme: 3
favourite parts: 1
who: 5
explain what: 2
extra note: 4

Exercise 2
1 False. 'Favourite parts' is missing.

2 False. The order in the answer is:
explain what: *I learned about the writer's life. I learned she was from a poor family. I learned she had no qualifications from school. Then she lived in different countries. I learned that she now lives in her hometown and she writes there.*
who: *I watched it with my classmates. We watched it at college in a seminar. Then we talked about her life.*
type of programme: *It was a documentary and it was about a famous writer. I enjoy reading her books. She writes about college students and their lives.*

3 False. The answer is out of order and incomplete.

Exercise 3
1 True

2 True

3 True

Exercise 4
Giving examples: A good example of this is; For example,
Organizing your answers: Firstly, Finally,

Part 3:   Exam practice

Part 1

Exercise 1

Model answers:
When did you last watch television?
I watched television yesterday. I finished my homework and I watched a couple of soap operas with my friends.

What do you usually watch on television?
I usually watch reality TV shows or game shows. I sometimes watch drama series too.

What are some popular programmes in your country?
TV is very popular in my country. There are lots of channels. Soap operas are very popular. Everybody watches them.

Why do you think some TV programmes are popular?
I think soap operas are popular because we like watching characters in real life. The characters are like friends or neighbours. It's good entertainment, because it is sometimes relaxing and sometimes exciting.

Part 2

Exercise 2

Model answer:
I'd like to talk about a TV programme I enjoy watching called *Chat Chat*.

It's a popular talk show and the guests are usually famous actors or singers. For example, two Oscar winners were on the show lat week.

Firstly, my favourite parts are the presenter and the music. The presenter is very funny and very good at is job. A good example of this is when he interviews guests. He is very kind and patient, so he can ask difficult questions and get honest answers. There is always a music part at the end of the show. A singer or group sing a song.

I usually watch this show on Saturday afternoons when I'm at my cousin's house. We love watching this show and we eat some snacks and just relax.

Finally, I enjoy watching this programme because it is funny, interesting and relaxing. I forget about my studies and my problems, and I enjoy learning about these famous people.

Unit 6   Weather

Part 1:   Language development

Vocabulary: The weather

Exercise 1
A rainy, wet

B cold, snowy

C stormy, windy

D hot, sunny

Exercise 2
A rainy, wet

B cold, snowy

C stormy, windy

D hot, sunny

Vocabulary: Talking about the weather

Exercise 4
1 favourite

2 it's

3 There's

4 lasts

5 makes

6 really like

Pronunciation: Vowel sounds

Exercise 7
u: humid, June
aʊ: drought, outside
ʌ: month, sunny
eɪ: April, rainy
ɔː: autumn, stormy
əʊ: November, snowy

Grammar: Can and can't

Exercise 9
1 can

2 can't

3 can't

4 can

5 can't

6 can

Exercise 11
1 season, it's, can, makes
  weather = extra

2 monsoon, for, can't, dry
  drought = extra

3 There's, can, from, thunderstorms
  stormy = extra

Part 2:   Skills development

Part 1

Exercise 1
1 a My country has four seasons. Answer b does not say *how many* seasons.

2 b Summer. This is my favourite season. Answer a is not relevant. The question is about the *season* not the type of *weather*.

3 a I feel very sad on rainy days. In Answer b, the speaker doesn't say *how* he/she feels.

4 b I like going to the beach. In Answer a, the speaker doesn't understand the question and the use of *like*. He/She thinks the question is *Do you like it when it's hot?*

Exercise 3
1 answer 2b

2 answer 1a

3 answer 4b

4 answer 3a

Exercise 5
b It doesn't include extra information.

Exercise 6
1 d

2 c

3 b

4 a

Exercise 7

Possible answers:

I'd like to describe my favourite type of weather. My country has three seasons and there are lots of types of weather. It is a difficult choice for me, but I think my favourite is wet weather. **I prefer this to the dry weather.**

Yes, wet weather is my favourite. I like going shopping when the weather is wet because the shops are all indoors. I also like cooking delicious meals for my family when there's lots of rain. **My favourite dish is a traditional meal with chicken and rice.**

I often experience this weather in other countries. I like travelling in Europe and I always take my umbrella with me. The wet weather lasts for a long time there. It is different from my country because the rainy season only lasts for two months. **It lasts from May to June.**

This weather is good for relaxing. For example, you can stay at home and just watch television. You can chat to your friends online too. **I speak to my friends for two or three hours.**

I really like the weather in spring. It's often warm but it is sometimes very hot. It's often cold too. There's lots of rain in spring. I like the different types of weather because you can't answer the question 'what's the weather like today?' We don't know!

It is different from other season in my country because it changes quickly. On Monday it's sunny, but on Tuesday there are thunderstorms. In summer, the weather is always hot. In autumn, the weather is usually cold and dry. In winter, it is always very cold and windy. Winter makes me feel sad.

The main reason why it is my favourite season is because there's lots of sun and you can do sports outside or just enjoy the warm weather with friends. Spring is also the end of winter which I don't like.

Part 3: Exam practice

Part 1

Exercise 1

Model answers

1 My country has four seasons.

2 The weather in my country is very dry. There's a rainy season in January and February.

3 I feel very sad on rainy days.

4 I like going to the beach when it's hot.

Part 2

Exercise 2

Model answer:

I'd like to describe my favourite season in my country. My country has four seasons and there are lots of types of weather. I think my favourite season is spring. I prefer this to the summer.

Spring lasts for about three months. It lasts from March to May. Some people think that spring is short and only lasts for about two months. Maybe this is true.

Review 2

Exercise 1

gallery, beach, bridge, café, factory, harbour, hotel, park, river, stadium, theatre, skyscraper

Exercise 2

1 d

2 c

3 b

4 e

5 a

Exercise 3

1 There is a harbour.

2 There are lots of people.

3 There isn't much traffic.

4 There aren't any markets.

5 There are two museums.

6 There isn't a beach.

7 There aren't any shopping malls.

8 There is a football stadium.

Exercise 4

Types of people: actors, characters, contestants, guests, participants, presenter

Types of programme: documentary, game show, news, reality TV show, soap opera, talk show

Exercise 5

1 about

2 set

3 presented

4 stars

5 good

6 best

Exercise 6

1 Matteo usually watches documentaries.

2 Matteo sometimes watches dramas.

3 Matteo rarely watches reality TV shows.

4 Matteo never watches soap operas.

Exercise 7

cold ≠ hot

drought ≠ monsoon

dry ≠ wet

rainy ≠ sunny

Exercise 8

1 season

2 for

3 rainy

4 feel

5 have

Exercise 9

1 can't

2 can

3 can

4 can't

5 can

6 can't

Unit 7 Studying

Part 1: Language development

Vocabulary: Academic subjects

Exercise 1

A computer science

B engineering

C mathematics

D medicine

Exercise 2

1 medicine, lectures, doctor

2 course, interesting, director

3 law, difficult, lawyer

Pronunciation: Word stress

Exercise 3

business 2
literature 3
mathematics 4
university 5

Exercise 4

1 [Oo]	2 [Ooo]	3 [ooOo]	4 [ooOoo]
business	literature	mathematics	university

Exercise 5

1 [Oo]	2 [Ooo]	3 [ooOo]	4 [ooOoo]
business	literature	mathematics	university
college	chemistry	engineering	
deadline	graduate	graduation	
lecture	history	presentation	
project	medicine		
	timetable		

Vocabulary: Collocations

Exercise 7

1 B

2 E

3 D

4 C

5 A

6 H

7 J

8 G

9 F

10 I

Exercise 8

1 results

2 university

3 year

4 presentations

5 essay

Grammar: Present continuous

Exercise 9

a Lara

b Marcel

c Dee

Exercise 10

now

Exercise 11

1 I'm revising for an exam. It's my final year and I'm working very hard. I'm having extra tuition and my grades are improving.

2 I'm visiting my brother at college. He's living in halls this year and he's having a great time. I'm helping him with his coursework this semester and we're preparing a presentation at the moment.

3 I'm thinking about doing another course next year. I'm applying for a scholarship at a university in my hometown and I'm filling out the application form now.

Part 2: Skills development

Part 2

Exercise 1

question 2

Exercise 2

1 T

2 T The answer includes friends and family and answers the question correctly.

3 T The speaker repeats nice three times.

Exercise 3

Yes, yes they are. My father and my brother studied law at university and they think it is a very <u>important</u> subject. My mother thinks it is <u>interesting</u> and always asks me question about law. I have lots of friends on the course and we want to get a <u>good</u> job when we graduate.

Exercise 4

1 T

2 T The answer includes friends and family and answers the question correctly.

3 F

Answer 3 is different. The speaker now uses a range of vocabulary.

Part 3

Exercise 7

a 2   c 1

b 3

Exercise 8

1 c   **3** b

2 a

Part 3: Exam practice

Part 1

Exercise 1

Model answers:
1 I'm studying Literature. I'm in my second year at university now.

2 I chose Literature because I love reading books and because I'd like to be a teacher.

3 Yes, the course is really interesting. I have great teachers and I like learning about new types of literature al the time.

4 That's interesting. There are lots of things I like. I think the best thing is going to lectures and learning about new topics.

5 I'm not sure. In my country, there are lots of good schools and colleges and I'd like to teach there. Or maybe I can apply for another course.

Part 2

Exercise 2

Model answers:
I'm going to talk about the subject I'm studying at university. I'm studying Literature.

The subject is about different types of literature from different times and from different countries.

For example, we learn about literature from Shakespeare's time to today's writers and modern literature. We go to the theatre to watch plays or we have seminars to talk about writers and novels. We're learning about American literature this semester which is really interesting.

I really enjoy the subject. I love reading books and now I can read new writers and experience different literature. I enjoy giving presentations and we do this every week on my course. Then we discuss our opinions. It's good fun.

Finally, I'm interested in the subject because I like learning about different times and different places and I can learn this from literature. We can learn about the world and about people. I think language is very beautiful and I enjoy reading different styles of writing.

Exercise 3

Model answers:
Yes, absolutely. I'd like to be a teacher. I'd like to work with school children and teach them about literature and about plays. I'd like a good job after my course. Or maybe I could write a book.

Part 3

Exercise 4

Model answers:
1 Yes, definitely. Children love meeting people and finding about new things. Unfortunately, some schools don't have good teachers and then the children don't enjoy school. But I think they always like learning and they can learn from their family or the internet. I enjoyed going to school when I was young.

2 Yes, absolutely. I live with my family. I enjoy living at home because I can relax and just study. For example, my parents cook meals, wash my clothes and clean my room. I can spend more time studying and I think this is good.

3 My parents went to a school in my hometown. The school is a very popular one and they enjoyed it. I went to school in anther country and I didn't like living away from home. My father went to university but I don't think there were lots of universities in my country at the time. Fortunately, there are lots of universities and colleges there today. I'm visiting different universities at the moment because I'm choosing which course to study next year.

4 Yes, definitely. You can learn about a new country and meet new people and I think we learn about life. It's very exciting. It's difficult to study in another language and it's hard work. But many students have extra tuition to help them and they learn the language of the country very quickly. Then the subject is easy and life is easy, I agree there are benefits but it's hard work.

Unit 8   Work

Part 1:   Language development

Vocabulary: Jobs

Exercise 1

A nurse

B journalist

C police officer

D teacher

Exercise 2

1 police officer

2 journalist

3 nurse

4 volunteer

5 businessman

6 teacher

Vocabulary: Your job

Exercise 6

1 b	3 c
2 a	4 b, c

Exercise 7

a part-time, applied, earning

b company, work experience, use my languages, flexible hours

c help people, travel the world, earning a good salary

Grammar: *Have to*

Exercise 9

1 have to

2 had to

3 didn't have to

4 don't have to

5 have to

6 have to

7 don't have to

8 have to

Exercise 12

1 as

2 to

3 for

4 well-known

5 use

6 well-paid

Part 2:   Skills development

Exercise 1

1 Compare your experience of finding a job to your parents' generation.

2 Many people think that work experience is the best way to learn about a job. What is your point of view?

3 In your opinion, do people work more now than in the past?

4 Do you think companies need people to travel to an office and work there, or can people work from home?

Exercise 2

a to give your opinion on an issue: 2, 4

b to compare past and present: 1, 3

Exercise 3

Question 2

Exercise 4

1 interesting

2 think

3 suppose …

4 cons

help the speaker = gives the speaker time to think and to relax

improve the answer = speak at a natural pace and without pauses

Exercise 5

Question 1

Exercise 6

1 interesting

2 see

3 guess

4 sure

5 disadvantages

Exercise 9

A Question 1: give your opinion on an issue
Question 2: compare the past to the present
useful phrases = all

Part 3: Exam practice

Part 1

Exercise 1

Model answers:
1 I'm a nurse. I work in a hospital near my home.

2 Yes, I enjoy my work. My job is great because I help people every day.

3 No, I don't think so. Maybe I can train as a chef because I like cooking.

4 I work for a private hospital. It is very well-known in my country. It is a friendly place to work. We get lots of training and we can work flexible hours. It's a good company.

5 Well, I work different shifts so I start work at different times. I get to the hospital and I talk to the other nurses about what we have to do that day. Then we visit all the patients and help them. I prepare food and medicine for the doctors.

Part 2

Exercise 2

Model answer:
I'd like to talk about a job I had in the past. When I was at college, I worked in an office as a receptionist.

I got the job because I applied for it. I saw an advert on a college notice board for a temporary receptionist. It was well-paid and the office was near the college. I emailed my CV and then I visited the office for an interview.

The job involved computer work and talking to people on the telephone. I liked using my languages and I enjoyed working with different people. I had to organize meetings and prepare reports. I sometimes visited another office and worked there.

I wanted the job because it was well-paid and I saved for a holiday. I also got work experience in a busy and exciting company and I think that's important. I leant a lot.

Finally, I did the job well. They gave me a good report for my college and they also brought me some flowers and a card to say thank you. I'd like to work there again.

Exercise 3

Model answers:

My colleagues were really nice. They were very friendly and helpful. My boss was friendly too.

Part 3

Exercise 4

Model answers:

1 That's an interesting question. In my opinion, I don't think it's a good idea for families to work together. For example, I have to work very hard in my job and I often feel sad or angry. But then I go home to my family and it's OK. It would be difficult if I had an argument at work, with my family, and then the argument continued at home.

2 Maybe. I think that work experience is very useful and you can learn a lot about the job. For example, maybe you don't like the job and want to look for a different career. I think it's also important to get a qualification and to go to college, then you can learn about background of the job.

3 Yes, definitely. We have computers and mobile phones and lots of people work from home today. It is normal. In the past, I think people travelled to a company and worked there, and then went home. All the work was done in the company. Today the world is very busy and people work more in their free time because they need money or because they have to work hard.

4 I'm not sure. I think it's a relaxing way to do a job because there aren't any noisy colleagues there. You can work flexible hours too which is good. But you need a big house and a desk and equipment, so it's difficult and expensive. Maybe it's a good idea to work at home for a day or two days but not every day.

Unit 9   Holidays and travel

Part 1:   Language development

Vocabulary: Holidays

Exercise 1
A beach holiday   C activity holiday

B coach tour   D safari

Exercise 2
do: new sports, water sports
eat in: traditional restaurants
go: sightseeing, swimming in the sea
go on: day trips
learn: new sports, water sports
take: lessons or a course
visit: tourist attractions, traditional restaurants
watch: local festivals

Vocabulary: Opposite adjectives

Exercise 4
1 d   3 e   5 b

2 f   4 c   6 a

Exercise 5
Possible answers

1 beautiful

2 comfortable / modern

3 exciting

4 delicious / disgusting

5 friendly / unfriendly

6 boring / friendly / unfriendly

7 comfortable / uncomfortable

Grammar: Future: *Be going to*

Exercise 6

1	learn new sports	✓
2	take lessons	✓
3	go swimming in the sea	✗
4	go sightseeing	✗
5	visit local festivals	✓
6	eat in traditional restaurants	✓
7	go on day trips	✓

Pronunciation: /ə/ and sentence stress

Exercise 9
1 with stress

2 no stress

Exercise 11
1 I'm <u>going</u> to <u>stay</u> in a hotel.

2 I'm <u>not</u> <u>going</u> to <u>take</u> any <u>photos</u>.

3 I'm <u>going</u> to <u>eat</u> in <u>traditional</u> <u>restaurants</u>.

4 We're <u>going</u> to <u>visit</u> <u>historical</u> <u>sites</u>.

5 We're <u>not</u> <u>going</u> to <u>learn</u> a <u>new</u> <u>sport</u>.

6 We're <u>going</u> to <u>go</u> <u>sightseeing</u>.

Part 2:   Skills development

Exercise 1
1 G   4 B   7 D

2 E   5 A   8 C

3 F   6 H

Exercise 8
1 C   3 O

2 O   4 C

Part 3:   Exam practice

Part 1
Exercise 1

Model answers:

1 My last holiday was last winter. I went on a family holiday to Australia.

2 Yes, I like travelling. I like visiting new countries or new places in my country, but I don't enjoy flying.

3 I like visiting friendly cities. I enjoy meeting new people and making new friends. I like old cities with traditional restaurants.

4 That's an interesting question. Yes, I'd like to visit Canada. I'd like to go skiing there.

5 No, I don't think so. Sadly, it's very expensive and the weather is bad. There are lots of tourist attractions and historical sites but the weather is always bad.

Part 2

Exercise 2

Model answers:

I'd like to talk about a special holiday I went on about two years ago. It was a learning holiday with my school.

Ten people from my class went to London in England and we went to take an English course at a university. It was about two years ago and it was in the summer. The course lasted for three weeks. We stayed in university halls and the beds were very uncomfortable.

We did lots of things. First of all, we studied very hard but we made lots of new friends. At the weekends, we went sightseeing and we visited tourist attractions. There are lots of beautiful places in London. I really enjoyed visiting the historical sites and going to the art galleries. We learnt new sports in the evenings. For example, we played cricket and rugby. Another thing we did was go on a day trip to Stratford to see a play by Shakespeare. It was a beautiful city but I didn't understand the play. We had an exam on the last day and thankfully I passed.

Finally, it's a special holiday because it was the first time I went on holiday without my family. It was also the first time I visited England and practised my English. It was very exciting.

Exercise 3

Model answer:

Yes, I'm going to do a language programme next year. I'm going to America and I'm going to work in a school for work experience.

Part 3

Exercise 4

Model answers:

1 I think travelling is very easy for my generation. It is cheap and quick to buy tickets on the internet and lots of people travel every day, for work or for holidays. But for my parents' generation, I think tickets were expensive and travelling wasn't very common. I don't think people went on long holidays to different countries, I think they probably stayed in their own country.

2 Yes, absolutely. My country is beautiful and the people are very friendly. Tourists come to my country every day so I think it's a good idea for us to visit the different areas of the country too. You can learn more about your country and its history and you can try local food or visit ancient ruins. I think it's a good idea.

3 That's interesting. I'm not sure. Most hotels or businesses speak lots of different languages so it's not important. Tourist attractions have guides that translate too. But it's polite to speak the language and to understand the people. I think it makes the visit more interesting.

4 Yes, absolutely. My favourite holidays or day trips are with my friends. Fortunately, we all have the same interests and like doing the same things and we can have a great time. I think it's nice to share experiences and take photos. It makes the trip special.

Review 3

Exercise 1
1 mathematics

2 engineering

3 medicine

4 computer science

5 history

6 law

Exercise 2
1 applying

2 giving

3 get

4 had

5 graduated

6 writing

Exercise 3
1 'm visiting

2 'm thinking

3 are improving

4 'm working

5 're preparing

6 'm learning

Exercise 4
1 journalist

2 volunteer

3 police officer

4 businessman

5 nurse

6 lawyer

7 teacher

8 chef

Exercise 5
1 earn

2 job

3 volunteer

4 hours

5 using

6 work

Exercise 6
1 have to

2 don't have to

3 had to

4 have to

5 don't have to

6 have to

Exercise 7
1 c	4 d
2 f	5 a
3 b	6 e

Exercise 8
beautiful ≠ horrible

comfortable ≠ uncomfortable

exciting ≠ boring

friendly ≠ unfriendly

modern ≠ traditional

Exercise 9
1 I'm going to learn new sports.

2 I'm not going to go swimming in the sea.

3 I'm going to go sightseeing.

4 I'm not going to visit local festivals.

5 I'm going to eat in traditional restaurants.

6 I'm going to take lots of photos.

Unit 10   Health

Part 1:   Language development

Vocabulary: Health

Exercise 1

A sleep for eight hours

B do sports

C eat well

D play board games

Exercise 2

Suggested answers:

good for your mind	good for your body	good for both

play board games
do yoga
draw pictures
play a musical
  instrument
play brain training
  games
	eat well
	do tae kwon do
	have a healthy diet
	play table tennis
		do sports
		sleep for eight
		  hours every
		  night

Exercise 3

1 doing yoga

2 brain training games

3 on my own

4 important to

5 makes me feel

6 good for

Vocabulary: Giving explanations

Exercise 5

Charles: chess, father
Rosa: cooking, family and friends

Exercise 6

1 hard

2 keep your mind active

3 happy

Exercise 7

It's: challenging / great / interesting / relaxing
It's important to: work in a team / relax after
   college / keep fit
It makes me feel: great / relaxed / healthy

Pronunciation: Contractions

Exercise 9

1 (It's) good for you.

2 It (isn't) good for you.

3 (It's) really bad for you.

4 (It's) important to stay healthy.

5 You (shouldn't) eat junk food.

Grammar: Should / shouldn't

Exercise 12

1 shouldn't	4 shouldn't
2 should	5 should
3 should	6 shouldn't

Part 2:   Skills development

Part 1

Exercise 1

1 a	3 a
2 a	4 b

Part 3

Exercise 4

1 b	2 a	3 c

Exercise 5

a question 2	c question 1
b question 3	

Exercise 6

1 Is the answer relevant?
   Answer a yes
   Answer b yes
   Answer c no – the student talks about different
      sports and sports he/he'd like to do.

2 What is the opinion, comparison or suggestion?
   Answer a suggestion: encourage young people
      to play outdoors and learn about food

Answer b opinion: important to slow and relax
Answer c comparison: not made

Exercise 9

1 opinion   3 comparison

2 suggestion

Part 3:   Exam practice

Part 1

Exercise 1

Model answers:
1 I like doing sports. My favourite sport is tennis. I enjoy playing tennis outdoors when it's hot.

2 It depends. Sometimes I watch important football games on TV. I prefer listening to sports on the radio or on my mobile.

3 Yes, I like playing golf. I always play at the weekend with my friends. I often go to the gym too. It's important to keep fit.

4 In my country, the most popular sport is football. Everybody loves it. Young boys play football every day and they'd like to be professional football players.

5 I spend four or five hours a week on my hobbies. I'd like to spend more time on my hobbies and interests, but my university course is very hard.

Part 2

Exercise 2

Model answers:
I'd like to describe an activity I like doing to keep healthy. The activity is yoga.

I really enjoy doing yoga. I do yoga every week and I do it in two different places. Firstly, I do yoga in my bedroom. Sometimes I do it after a hard day at university but I usually do it in the morning. Secondly, I do yoga at a yoga centre near university.

In my opinion, it keeps me healthy in different ways. It is good for my body because I have to be strong and fit. It's really challenging! It is good for my mind too, because I have to focus my mind on one thing. It's good to forget about studying and exams when you are tired.

Finally, I like doing it because it's important to keep fit and it makes me feel very relaxed and calm. I don't like going to gyms or noisy places, so doing yoga at home or in a quiet class is great.

Exercise 3

Model answers:
1 No. My sister likes doing tae kwon do. She tried yoga but she didn't like it. My brother prefers playing football or cricket. He likes team sports.

2 Yes, I'd like to do yoga every day. I'm going to do more yoga after my exams finish. In fact, I'm going on a yoga holiday in the summer.

Part 3

Exercise 4

Model answers:
1 That's an interesting question. There are lots of differences between sports now and in the past. I think money is one big difference. For example, big companies sponsor some sports competitions and competitors can win lots of money. Technology is another difference. For example, motor racing is different compared to the past. Today the cars are very fast and drivers often make new records.

2 I'm not sure. I think some people eat better because they have lots of money. They can buy different fresh food or they can go to the best restaurants. Cooking is a popular hobby for some people. But there are lots of poor people in my country and they don't eat well. For example, they have to eat cheap food or junk food and this is bad for them.

3 That's interesting. Firstly, I think we should encourage young people to be healthy. It's important to stay healthy. We should use the media and famous people to encourage young people. For example, TV shows can show people exciting sports. Famous people can describe activities or healthy diets. Finally, parents should show their children how to be healthy.

4 Yes, definitely. In my opinion, I think the government should teach people about healthy lifestyles. For example, give people information about healthy diets so people can eat well. They should describe different activities that are good for your mind and for your body. Then people in the country can be fit and happy and healthy.

Unit 11   Important events

Part 1:   Language development

Vocabulary: Important events

Exercise 1
A graduating from university

B getting married

C travelling on your own for the first time

D winning a sports competition
   extra = coming of age, getting your first job

Exercise 2
1 travelling on his own for the first time

2 parents

3 very nervous, very excited

Vocabulary: Describing feelings

Exercise 4

negative feelings	positive feeliings
bored/boring terrified/terrifying tired/tiring	delighted excited/exciting relaxed/relaxing satisfied/satisfying surprised/surprising

Exercise 5
terrified, boring, tired, surprised, relaxed, tiring,
   delighted, satisfied, exciting

Exercise 6
1 terrified

2 boring

3 tired

4 surprised

5 relaxed

6 tiring

7 delighted

8 satisfied

9 exciting

Pronunciation: Giving emphasis

Exercise 7
really and *very*

Grammar: Comparing

Exercise 9
1 c	3 a
2 d	4 b

Exercise 10
1 most

2 more

3 better than

4 more

5 most

6 happier

7 more

Exercise 12
1 the

2 younger

3 nervous extra = most

4 wasn't

5 boring

6 happier

7 than

8 felt

Part 2:   Skills development

Part 1

Exercise 1
1 b Answer a uses the present simple (*I play*) but
      the question is about events in the past. The
      answer has to include a past tense.

2 a Answer b uses the present continuous (*I'm
      using*) but the question is about habits that
      are repeated in the present. The answer has
      to be the present simple.

3 a Answer b doesn't include the *to* in *going to.*
      The answer has to include the correct form
      of *(to be) going to.*

4 b Answer a uses *since* with a period of time. *For* is correct with a period of time and *since* is correct with a point in time, e.g. since 2011.The present perfect is practised in Unit 12.

Exercise 2

1 a   4 b

2 b   5 a

3 b

Part 2

Exercise 5

Past simple
There was/were
Present perfect

Exercise 6

present simple
past simple
present perfect
should
there was/were

Part 3

Exercise 8

1 have to

2 meet, is

3 more difficult

4 're starting

5 're going to

Part 3:   Exam practice

Part 1

Exercise 1

Model answers:
1 Yes, I have a large family. There is my mother, my father, four brothers and one sister. My parents are from big families too, so I've got lots of cousins.

2 Yes, my favourite teacher at school was Mrs Holder. She was very kind and she taught English and French. Everybody enjoyed her lessons. She was clever and funny.

3 Yes, I'm a creative person, so I enjoy making things. For example, I like drawing pictures or making cakes. I make lots of traditional food and I like eating out at restaurants.

4 My hometown is very small. It's near the border and it's very pretty. There's a beach and a harbour. There aren't many shops or offices. It's very friendly and it's famous for the old bridge in the town centre.

5 I've been to lots of countries. I've been to Europe three or four times. I've been to America and I've been to Australia. I really enjoy travelling. I think it's important to learn about other countries.

Part 2

Exercise 2

Model answers:
I'd like to describe an important event in my life. I'd like to describe my graduation from high school.

This took place in 2010 and in my hometown. I live near my school and my father went to the school. My grandfather went to the school too and my mother taught there when I was young. It's important to my family. The graduation didn't happen at the school. It happened at the town hall. It's a beautiful, old building and it opens for special occasions.

My family were there. All of my friends from school were there. There were some important people from the town too. They made a speech and gave me the graduation certificate.

Finally, it was important to me for lots of different reasons. Firstly, my grandparents live in another town but they made the trip to see my graduation. I was surprised to see them. Secondly, I had extra tuition in my final year at school and it was very challenging for me. I felt really satisfied when I passed my exams. Finally, it was my birthday too, so I got lots of presents. It was one of the best days of my life.

Exercise 3

Model answers:
1 Definitely. Life is very busy and it's important to remember special days. It's good to talk about it with your family and friends and look at photos of the event. It makes me feel very happy.

2 That's a difficult question. Let me think. I think planned events are more enjoyable because planned events are usually bigger and more important. For example, a graduation ro a wedding.

Part 3

Exercise 4

Model answers:
1 That's interesting. Let me see. Firstly, I think people are getting married when they are older now. People got married really young in my parents' generation. In my opinion, I think organizing events is very different. Today we can plan things using the internet at home, but in the past people spent lots of time travelling to shops or places to discuss events.

2 That's an interesting question. There are lots of ways to remember important events. I think people should remember the most important events by learning about the event and then going to a celebration each year. In my country, we have parades or festivals to remember important events. I think this is a good way.

3 In my country, sports and exams are very important. For example, there are lots of schools with special departments that teach sports and the teachers are sometimes professional sports people. I think all schools organize lots of extra tuition to help students before exams. I had problems in my last year at school and I had extra classes to help me. It's important to work hard.

4 Yes, definitely. I've got lots of photos on my mobile and on my laptop. They make me feel happy and they remind me of a special day or a funny day. It's one of the best ways to remember special occasions. Some people like making videos of the special occasion or buying gifts. I think these are good but in my opinion photos are the best.

Unit 12   Possessions

Part 1:   Language development

Vocabulary: Objects

Exercise 3

Size	age	colour	material
large	modern	black	glass
small	new	red	leather
	old-fashioned	green	metal
			plastic
			silver
			wood

Exercise 4

1 guitar: modern, red, silver, wood, plastic

2 handbag: large, old-fashioned, red, leather

Vocabulary: Describing objects

Exercise 6

1 e	3 a	5 b
2 c	4 f	6 d

Exercise 7

1 I use it for

2 It reminds me of

3 It's important to me because

4 it's made of

Pronunciation: Linking words

Exercise 9

1 It's made of leather.

2 I use it for texting my friends.

3 I like it because

4 It's important to me because

5 It reminds me of

Grammar: Present perfect with *for* and *since*

Exercise 11

1 had, for

2 owned, since

3 used, for

4 carried, since

5 worn, for

6 wanted, since

Exercise 13

1 possessions

2 favourite

3 it

4 had

5 bought

6 modern

7 important

8 reminds

9 wear

   extra = carry, green

Part 2:   Skills development

Exercise 1

1 pause, natural

2 notes

3 organize

Exercise 3

1 tenses

2 carefully, choose

Exercise 5

1 topic

2 repeat, describing

3 similar, adverbs

Exercise 7

1 model, repeat

2 pronunciation, stress

3 suitable

4 clearly

Part 3: Exam practice

Part 1

Exercise 1

Model answers:
1 I'm from China. My hometown is Beijing. I've lived there since I was a baby.

2 The most popular place to go shopping in my hometown is the shopping mall near the stadium. It's really big and has lots of different shops and cafes.

3 I rarely shop online. I like going to shops and looking at things. I sometimes buy music online.

4 I bought a present for my best friend last week. I bought her a silver necklace for her birthday. She was very surprised.

5 I like visiting galleries and museums. I really enjoy meeting friends for coffee and chatting. It's very relaxing.

Part 2

Exercise 2

Model answers:
I'd like to describe something which is very important to me. The possession is my mobile phone.

It's very small, modern and red and silver. I think it's made of metal and plastic. It looks great. It's very fashionable and expensive too. I carry it in my bag every day

I've had it for six months. I got it when I was on holiday in England. It reminds me of my holiday and the rainy weather. I've used it every day since I bought it. I use it to download apps and listen to music. I text or call my family with it. I can use the internet and I can organize my diary. I can do everything with it. It's really good.

Finally, it's important to me because it's my connection with my family. Now I'm living and studying in another country, I rarely see my family. I can make video calls with my phone and see my parents. It makes me feel happy.

Exercise 3

Model answers:
1 Yes, there are lots of mobile phones in shops. I can go to the shopping mall

tomorrow and buy a new mobile phone. I enjoy shopping so it would be fun.

2 Yes, absolutely. I think my mobile phone is one of the best phones. My best friend likes my mobile, because its' smaller than his mobile phone.

Part 3

Exercise 4

Model answers:
1 That's an interesting question. It depends. I think possessions can make people happy, yes. For example, you're working really hard for your exams and then someone buys you a 'good luck' present, I think that would make people happy. Lots of people own expensive objects but they feel sad. In my opinion, I think friends and family make people happier than objects.

2 My most important possession is probably my mobile phone. I always carry it in my bag and I use it every day. I think my parents' important possessions are probably big things like cars or houses. I think family photos are probably more important to my mother. I suppose young people think modern, electrical things are more important than big, expensive objects.

3 Yes, absolutely. I love shopping. It's a relaxing activity for me and I spend lots of my free time going to the shopping mall. It's relaxing because you can meet your friends and go shopping together. I like shopping online too. When the shopping mall is very busy or when you are really tired, you can look online and then buy things.

4 That's interesting. Let me see. I really enjoy giving presents to people. I like thinking about the present, buying it and wrapping it. When the person opens the present, it makes me feel satisfied. But I like getting presents too. I got this coat for my birthday and I've worn it every day since my birthday. I think it's better to receive a present.

Review 4

Exercise 1
1 sports

2 yoga

3 well

4 healthy

5 musical

6 games

7 brain

8 hours

Exercise 2
1 keep your mind active

2 challenging

3 keep fit

Exercise 3
a 3, 6   b 2, 5   c 1, 4

Exercise 4
1 come

2 get

3 get

4 graduate

5 travel

6 win

Exercise 5

positive feelings:	delighted, excited, happy, relaxed, satisfied
negative feelings:	bored, nervous, terrified, tired

Exercise 6
1 are

2 than

3 more

4 is

5 the

Exercise 7
1 A large, brown, leather coat.

2 A small, modern, plastic mobile phone.

3 A new, red, metal watch.

4 A small, old-fashioned, green, necklace.

Exercise 8
1 made

2 for

3 got

4 important

5 use

6 me

Exercise 9
1 I've **owned** it for five years.

2 **I've** wanted a phone since I was ten years old.

3 I've **worn** it every day since I got it.

4 I've **used** my computer for two years.

5 I've had it **for** three years.

6 **I've carried** it in my bag since my graduation.

7 I've **been** to England three times.

8 correct

Practice test

Part 1

Model answers:

1 I'm a student. I'm studying medicine and I'm in my second year at university. And I study English too. It's my favourite subject.

2 No, I'm an only child, so I don't have any brothers or sisters. But I have lots of cousins and aunts and uncles, because my parents have lots of brothers and sisters. I have three nephews too.

3 My hometown is very big. It's very busy and dirty. There are lots of cars and there's lots of traffic. But the people are really friendly and it's a good city for tourists. You can go to the beach, you can go shopping or you can eat in a traditional restaurant.

4 It's always hot and sunny. I think tourists enjoy the weather. We have a rainy season and this lasts for about two months. I don't like the rainy season, because it makes me feel sad.

5 In my country, football is very popular and it's my favourite hobby. I love playing football with my friends. We play in competitions every weekend. I enjoy watching sports programmes on TV too. I also like going to the gym or going jogging, but sometimes I like doing nothing or watching films with my cousins. It's important to relax.

Part 2

Model answers:
I'd like to describe a person who helped me. I'm going to talk about a teacher from my high school. Her name was Mrs. White.

I met Mrs. White on my first day at school. I felt very nervous because I didn't know anyone. My family moved to the city about one month before school term, so I didn't have any friends. She talked to my parents and then we walked to her classroom. I sat at a table with two funny boys. We've been friends since my first day.

Mrs. White was a very friendly and kind person. She always listened to students and helped them. She was a great teacher and her lessons were very interesting. It made me feel confident about studying.

I think she was special because she liked everybody in her class. She encouraged everybody to work hard and to think about jobs and careers. But she was really funny and the class had fun too.

Finally, Mrs. White helped me because she encouraged me to apply for a university course. She helped me with my application form and she organized a scholarship for me. She was great.

Yes, I'd like to help someone in this way. I think it's important to help others. Actually, I'm training to be a teacher, so I'm going to help lots of children. I'm going to graduate in the summer, then I'm going to work in a school in my hometown. I'm very excited.

Part 3

Model answers:

1 Yes, definitely. In my opinion, we can learn lots of things from older generations. Firstly, we can learn about history or tradition and what happened in the past. Secondly, we can listen to advice from people with lots of experience. Finally, I think it's important to listen to a different opinion because it helps people to understand the world.

2 That's an interesting question. Let me think. I think today's family rarely live together. People live and work all over the world. Families often don't live in the same town or country. I'm not sure, but I think families lived together in the past. In my opinion, I think it was easier for families to help family members in the past. It is harder when people live in another place.

3 That's a very difficult question. I'm not sure. I think families should help but we should be independent too. It depends. I think we should ask families for help with big problems, because they can give advice or money. But I think we should try being independent with smaller problems.

4 In my country, we have a coming-of-age ceremony on your eighteenth birthday. This is when you're going to be an adult. It's a very important occasion and we celebrate it with family and friends. But I think some people become adults after they are eighteen. For example, when you are independent and live in another country, or when you get married.

Glossary

Key

adj. = adjective

n. = noun

v. = verb

Unit 1

bossy **adj.** – A bossy person enjoys telling other people what to do.

brother **n.** – Your brother is a boy or man who has the same parents as you.

calm **adj.** – Someone who is calm is quiet and does not show any worry or excitement.

clever **adj.** – intelligent and quick to understand things

confident **adj.** – People who are confident are sure of their own abilities or qualities.

creative **adj.** – Creative people are able to invent and develop original ideas.

daughter **n.** – Someone's daughter is their female child.

friendly **adj.** – If you are friendly to someone, you behave in a kind and pleasant way to them.

funny **adj.** – causing amusement or laughter

grandparent **n.** – Your grandparents are your parents' parents.

happy **adj.** – feeling, showing, or producing contentment or pleasure

husband **n.** – A woman's husband is the man she is married to.

kind **adj.** – Someone who is kind is considerate and generous towards other people.

mother **n.** – Your mother is the woman who gave birth to you.

parent **n.** – Your parents are your father and mother.

sister **n.** – Your sister is a girl or woman who has the same parents as you.

son **n.** – Someone's son is their male child.

wife **n.** – A man's wife is the woman he is married to.

Unit 2

boring **adj.** – dull and lacking interest

exciting **adj.** – making you feel happy and enthusiastic

interesting **adj.** – making you want to know, learn or hear more

Unit 3

cake **n.** – a sweet food made by baking flour, eggs, fat, and sugar

card **n.** – a piece of stiff paper or plastic with information or a message on it

carnival **n.** – a public festival with music, processions, and dancing

costume **n.** – a set of clothes worn by an actor

dance **v.** – To dance means to move your feet and body rhythmically in time to music.

eat **v.** – To eat means to chew and swallow food.

family **n.** – a group consisting of parents and their children; also all the people who are related to each other, including aunts and uncles, cousins, and grandparents

fireworks **n.** – small containers of gunpowder and other chemicals which explode or produce coloured sparks or smoke when lit

parade **n.** – a line of people or vehicles standing or moving together as a display

present **n.** – something that you give to someone for them to keep

visit **v.** – If you visit someone, you go to see them and spend time with them.

wear **v.** – When you wear something such as clothes, make-up, or jewellery, you have them on your body or face.

Unit 4

airport **n.** – a place where people go to catch planes

beach **n.** – an area of sand or pebbles beside the sea

beautiful **adj.** – very attractive or pleasing

bridge **n.** – a structure built over a river, road, or railway so that vehicles and people can cross

busy **adj.** – A busy place is full of people doing things or moving about.

café **n.** – a place where you can buy light meals, snacks, and drinks

factory **n.** – a building or group of buildings where goods are made in large quantities

gallery **n.** – a building or room where works of art are shown

harbour **n.** – a protected area of deep water where boats can be moored

market **n.** – a place where goods or animals are bought and sold

modern **adj.** – relating to the present time

museum **n.** – a building where many interesting or valuable objects are kept and displayed

park **n.** – a public area with grass and trees

river **n.** – a natural feature consisting of water flowing for a long distance between two banks

shopping mall **n.** – a large building that contains a lot of shops all close to each other

skyscraper **n.** – a very tall building

theatre **n.** – a building where plays and other entertainments are performed on a stage

Unit 5

actor **n.** – a man or woman whose job is acting in plays, television, or films

character **n.** – The characters in a film, play, or book are the people in it.

contestant **n.** – The contestants in a competition are the people taking part in it.

documentary **n.** – a radio or television programme, or a film, which provides information on a particular subject

drama series **n.** – a television series which tells a serious story over several episodes

game show **n.** – a television show in which contestants play a game, often to win money

guest **n.** – someone, especially a famous person, who is interviewed on a television show

presenter **n.** – someone who introduces a television programme

reality TV show **n.** – a television show which shows ordinary people doing tasks and reacting to each other

series **n.** – a set of radio or television programmes with the same title

soap opera **n.** – a popular television drama serial about people's daily lives

the news **n.** – a television or radio programme which gives information about things that are happening in the world

Unit 6

autumn **n.** – the season between summer and winter

cold **adj.** – having a low temperature

dry season **n.** – the time of year in some parts of the world when there is very little rain

hot **adj.** – having a high temperature

last **v.** – If something lasts, it continues to exist or happen.

monsoon season **n.** – the time of year in some parts of the world when there is very heavy rain

rain **n.** – water falling from the clouds in small drops

rainy **adj.** – When it is rainy, there is a lot of rain.

snowy **adj.** – When it is snowy, there is snow.

spring **n.** – Spring is the season between winter and summer.

stormy **adj.** – When it is stormy, there is heavy rain and strong winds.

summer **n.** – Summer is the season between spring and autumn.

sunny **adj.** – When it is sunny, the sun is shining.

thunderstorm **n.** – a storm in which there is thunder and lightning

wet **adj.** – If something is wet, it is covered in water or another liquid.

windy **adj.** – If it is windy, there is a lot of wind.

winter **n.** – Winter is the season between autumn and spring.

Unit 7

art **n.** – Art is the creation of objects such as paintings and sculptures, which are thought to be beautiful or which express a particular idea; also used to refer to the objects themselves

business studies **n.** – the study of how to set up and manage businesses

computer science **n.** – the study of computers and computer programming

engineering **n.** – Engineering is the profession of designing and constructing machinery and electrical devices, or roads and bridges.

history **n.** – History is the study of the past. A history is a record of the past.

law **n.** – The law is the system of rules developed by the government of a country, which regulate what people may and may not do and deals with people who break these rules.

linguistics **n.** – Linguistics is the study of language and of how it works.

literature **n.** – Literature consists of novels, plays, and poetry.

mathematics **n.** – Mathematics is the study of numbers, quantities, and shapes.

medicine **n.** – Medicine is the treatment of illness and injuries by doctors and nurses.

Unit 8

businessman **n.** – a man who works in business

chef **n.** – a head cook in a restaurant or hotel

lawyer **n.** – a person who is qualified in law, and whose job is to advise people about the law and represent them in court

nurse **n.** – a person whose job is to look after people who are ill

police officer **n.** – a member of the police

personal assistant **n.** – someone who works for a senior person in an organization, and helps them do their job

teacher **n.** – a person who teaches other people, especially children

volunteer **n.** – someone who does work for which they are not paid

Unit 9

activity holiday **n.** – a holiday during which you do sports or other physical activities

beach holiday **n.** – a holiday during which you spend a lot of time relaxing on a beach

city break **n.** – a short holiday to a city

coach tour **n.** – a tour of an area, travelling on a bus

cruise **n.** – a holiday in which you travel on a ship and visit places

day trip **n.** – a journey for pleasure to a place and back again on the same day

honeymoon **n.** – a holiday taken by a couple who have just got married

safari **n.** – an expedition for hunting or observing wild animals

water sports **n.** – sports that you play in water

Unit 10

challenging **adj.** – difficult in a way that is interesting and enjoyable

interesting **adj.** – making you want to know, learn or hear more

relax **v.** – If you relax, you become calm and your muscles lose their tension.

relaxed **adj.** – calm and not worried or tense

relaxing **adj.** – making you feel calm and not worried or tense

Unit 11

bored **adj.** – If you are bored, you are impatient because you do not find something interesting or because you have nothing to do.

boring **adj.** – dull and lacking interest

delighted **adj.** – extremely pleased and happy

excited **adj.** – happy and unable to relax

exciting **adj.** – making you feel happy and enthusiastic

relaxed **adj.** – calm and not worried or tense

satisfied **adj.** – happy because you have got what you want

satisfying **adj.** – Something that is satisfying gives you a feeling of pleasure and fulfilment.

surprised **adj.** – If you are surprised, you have a feeling of surprise because something unexpected has happened.

surprising **adj.** – unusual or unexpected

terrified **adj.** – extremely frightened

terrifying **adj.** – making you feel extremely frightened

tired **adj.** – having little energy

tiring **adj.** – Something that is tiring makes you tired.

Unit 12

black **adj. n.** – Black is the darkest possible colour, like tar or soot.

glass **n.** – Glass is a hard, transparent substance that is easily broken, used to make windows and bottles.

green **adj. n.** – Green is a colour between yellow and blue on the spectrum.

large **adj.** – Someone or something that is large is much bigger than average.

leather **n.** – Leather is the tanned skin of some animals, used to make shoes and clothes.

metal **n.** – Metal is a chemical element such as iron, steel, copper, or lead. Metals are good conductors of heat and electricity and form positive ions.

modern **adj.** – relating to the present time

new **adj.** – recently made, created, or discovered

old-fashioned **adj.** – Something which is old-fashioned is no longer fashionable.

photo **n.** – a photograph

plastic **n.** – a substance made by a chemical process that can be moulded when soft to make a wide range of objects

red **n. adj.** – Red is the colour of blood or of a ripe tomato.

silver **adj. n.** – greyish–white

small **adj.** – Small means not large in size, number, or amount.

smart phone **n.** – a mobile phone on which you can make phone calls and send texts, and also use the internet

wood **n.** – Wood is the substance which forms the trunks and branches of trees.

Pronunciation chart

In this book the International Phonetic Alphabet (IPA) is used to show how some words are pronounced. The symbols used in the International Phonetic Alphabet are shown in the table below.

IPA Symbols

Vowel	Sounds	Consonant	Sounds
ɑ	calm, ah	b	bed, rub
æ	act, cat	d	done, red
aɪ	dive, cry	f	fit, if
aɪə	fire, tyre	g	good, dog
aʊ	out, down	h	hat, horse
aʊə	flour, sour	j	yellow, you
e	met, lend, pen	k	king, pick
eɪ	say, weight	l	lip, bill
eə	fair, care	m	mat, jam
ɪ	fit, win	n	not, tin
i	seem, me	p	pay, lip
ɪə	near, beard	r	run, read
ɒ	lot, spot	s	soon, bus
əʊ	note, coat	t	talk, bet
ɔ	raw, more	v	van, love
ɔɪ	boy, joint	w	win, wool
ʊ	could, stood	x	loch
u	you, use	z	zoo, buzz
ʊə	cure, pure	ʃ	ship, wish
ɜ	turn, third	ʒ	measure, television
ʌ	fund, must	ŋ	sing, working
ə	about	tʃ	cheap, witch
		θ	thin, earth
ː	*lengthens the vowel sound*	ð	then, bathe
		dʒ	joy, bridge

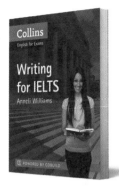

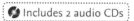

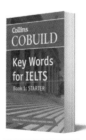

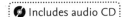

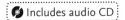